✱ Answer to the question on the cover:
Robert Reed (Mike Brady) did not appear in episode 116, the last one.

The Brady Bunch Files

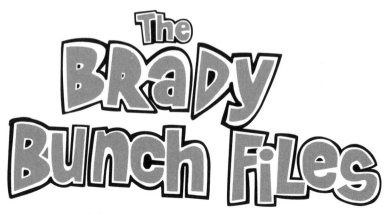

The Brady Bunch Files

1,500 BRADY TRIVIA QUESTIONS GUARANTEED TO DRIVE YOU BANANAS!

Lauren Johnson

RENAISSANCE BOOKS
Los Angeles

Library of Congress Catalog Card Number: 00-108840
ISBN: 1-58063-165-7

10 9 8 7 6 5 4 3 2 1

Design by Amanda Tan
Typesetting by Geoffrey Bock

Published by Renaissance Books
Distributed by St. Martin's Press
Manufactured in the United States of America
First edition

Acknowledgments

There are so many people I'd like to acknowledge for their part in all this, however, before I do so, let me say that *none* of this would have even been possible if it weren't for Sherwood Schwartz, an extraordinary man whose creative genius has inspired me in more ways than I can count, and for that I'll be eternally grateful. Sherwood is undoubtedly one of *the* nicest people on this planet, and I am so incredibly honored to call him my friend.

In addition to my undying gratitude for the entire *Brady Bunch* (which goes without saying), I would also like to thank my own *bunch* (Mom, Dad, Kirsten, Reid, and Curt) for all their love and support, especially my parents, Lynn and Noel, who never took away my TV privileges in their entirety, even when I was behaving in a most un-*Brady*-like fashion. I'd also like to thank my sister Kirsten for putting up with the endless *Brady*-babble and late-night phone calls, especially considering I'm on Pacific time and she's not. And lastly, there's Spot and Mac who continue to love me even though I'm forever screaming at them for stepping all over the keyboard-dddddddddddddd while I'm trying to write.

I would also like to extend a very special thanks to my very good friend, Marty Krofft, truly an angel in disguise and without whom this book would not be a *real* book . . . *and* without whom life wouldn't be nearly as much fun. And speaking of fun . . . I'd also like to acknowledge Marty's three wonderful daughters, Deanna, Kristina, and especially my *little* Soul Sister, Kendra, who keeps me laughing and feeling sane.

I also owe a debt of gratitude to Abbey Park and Mike Dougherty at Renaissance Media for believing in this book *and* for being so patient. I also want to extend a humungous thanks to Kerry McCluggage at Paramount, and his assistant Kimberly Koenen, for getting the ball rolling and doing such a wonderful thing.

A few others whose support and encouragement have meant the world to me: Suzae Johnson and Ed Underhill, MaryBeth Czsma, Larry Hines, Greg Witek, Jean Scott, Alice Johnson, Maria Roca Besso, Audrey Boston, Nancy Moore, Anne-Sophie and Jean-François LaCoste-Bourgeacq, Catherine Milord, Alex Govostis, Peter Andrews, Michael Croydon, Linda Kaari Predskaya, Walter Patton, Ursula Gabel, Kim Stevenson, Brooke Covington, Kim Jackson, Alessa Carlino, Joy Quanrud, Laurie Scheer, Jill Richling, Lori Mayfield, Mary Fitzgerald, Andy Besser, and Craig Fenter. I'd also like to thank Joe Hubbell for his love and support *and* for helping to make this so easy.

And then there's the Starbucks crowd . . .

Three more thanks that *must* be said, although two are no longer with us and the other is all around us: Allan Carr, Bill W., and the Big Man Upstairs.

Contents

The Brady Bunch Files

Part One

The Introduction

I know, I know . . . one thousand five hundred trivia questions is a bit much, but you know, when you think about all the other things in this world I could overindulge in (drugs and alcohol to name a few), one tiny, minor obsession with America's favorite family is hardly anything to worry about.

Well . . . maybe there's cause for a *little* concern when I find myself wondering what Carol Brady would do . . . like the time my ex-husband and I were home sick with the measles shortly after we were married and I wasn't sure which doctor to call—*his or mine?* I thought to myself "Hmmm . . . if Mike and Carol Brady can each keep their own doctors, then why can't we?" Or the time I promised my Garden Club I could get *Aerosmith* to perform at our Annual Ladies Luncheon because I was president of their fan club. But when their manager called to say they couldn't break away from their tour for me, the *president* of their fan club, I was so humiliated I just couldn't tell the ladies we had no entertainment because I was afraid I wouldn't be *popular*. But, like a good Brady, I came clean.

So, although my obsession with America's favorite family may not be the healthiest, devoting my life to driving people nuts as they desperately try to recall who sleeps on the top bunk is, by comparison to most any other popular vice, good, clean fun.

Why do I think anyone cares? What made me think that anyone would want to spend their hard-earned cash on hundreds of pages of useless information? I'll tell you why. Because so many of us privately pride ourselves in our ability to, without hesitation, recall that it was Peter who slept on the top bunk, yet the shame in being so Brady-literate can sometimes be too much for us. Buying this book could be the first step in coming out of the closet for many of us. A symbolic gesture of sorts in letting our friends and family know that we love the Bradys and we're not afraid to admit it.

It all started in the fall of 1982, my freshman year in college. That's when I realized the deep, dark secret I'd kept for so many years, the secret I'd guarded with my life for fear of being found out was simply a cultural norm. I was no longer an anomaly. I was free at last.

Everyone who was anyone knew *something* about this celebrated family—from the color of the kitchen counters to the Fillmore Junior High fight song, from where Marcia hid her diary to whose hair turned orange the night before graduation. For some bizarre reason, these silly details have been implanted in the collective consciousness of those who were weaned on it. But why? How is it most of us can't even remember our own phone numbers or a person's name two minutes after we've been introduced, but we can remember the Bradys live at 4222 Clinton Way and that Alice's sisters' names are Emily and Myrtle?

The answer to this question, which has until now perplexed me to no end is . . . well . . . quite simple—we keep watching it. But *why* do we keep watching it? What do we think is going to happen? That somehow, this time, something will be different? That maybe Greg won't stop at the newsstand to check out hot rod magazines where he loses Mike's important sketches? That Peter will remember Mom always says, "Don't play ball in the house" and think before throwing the basketball that shatters her favorite vase? I don't think so. Could it be because the entire family represents a variety of ages and marital statuses (divorced, widowed, remarried, single, dating, too young to date), providing a little something for everyone? I don't think so. Then perhaps it's the sexual tension we all wondered about. After all, the boys weren't *really* related to the girls, and the only thing separating them at night was a single bathroom. But although that may have been what attracted us as pre-pubescents, I seriously doubt it has anything to do with why we keep coming back today. So then what's the deal with this family that just won't go away? What is it that drives us to continually torture ourselves with bad perms, corny jokes, and long-winded lectures on the virtues of "one for all and all for one"?

It's simple. I believe it's the very normal need for control. And there's definitely a sense of control knowing ahead of time that Marcia's going to get nailed in the nose by a football. It's simply knowing what's going to happen *before* it happens. If we know ahead of time that Bobby does get to meet Joe Namath before the end of the episode, we don't have to spend the first twenty minutes stressing out along with the rest of the Bradys. Or to know that Carol will get her voice back in time to sing in church on Christmas morning, so we can sit back and enjoy the show. In fact, we can check our brains at the door. This type of activity requires no thinking, no feeling. That's the beauty of it. So, although most of us feel out of control in our daily lives, watching The Brady Bunch allows us a thirty-minute reprieve from the chaos and uncertainties of daily living.

And to have a forum, such as this book, in which we can test the limits of our Brady knowledge, we are validated and empowered, and the shame becomes nothing more than a faint memory . . . but then, what do I know? Who am I to say what lurks in the minds of Bradymaniacs? I'm as crazy as the rest of them.

Sherwood Schwartz struck gold when he decided to bring together six kids of various ages, as well as a widower, a possible divorcee (it never *was* made clear what exactly happened to Carol's first husband), and a nutty house-keeper. In doing so, *The Brady Bunch* would appeal to a mass audience.

Much like Mr. Schwartz, I figured the success of my project would depend largely on the size of my audience. There are three difficulty levels: One, for those who watched *The Brady Bunch* in the seventies; two, for those who *continued* to watch in the eighties; and three, for those who are *still* watching into the new millennium.

While reading this book, it's important to understand how it works. It isn't meant to be read cover to cover. You must decide which difficulty level is right for you and stick to those questions. You see, some of the questions are basically the same, however, the *difficulty level* will determine just how much information is supplied. For example, a level one question may read: Whose voice changed shortly before *The Brady Six* were supposed to record their first hit song? A level two question might read: Who said, "Of all the crummy times for my voice to change"? And a level three question may read: What was Peter referring to when he said, "Of all the crummy times for my voice to change"? You may remember it was Peter whose voice changed during one particular episode, but you might not remember why it was such a crummy time for it to change.

The answers will contain more information and basically set up the scenario in which the situation occurred, no matter what the difficulty level. The answer will also include the corresponding episode name and number, which can then be easily looked up in the Episode Guide to further refresh your memory if necessary.

You might also read the questions to other people and vice versa. Keep a tally going. It's up to you to decide how exact an answer must be. A great game idea is to score points by difficulty level. It's up to the player to decide which difficulty level he wants (let *him* choose the question number). If he asks for a level three, but he's fallen a little behind, he might end up with nothing. And if you're a level one and you're feeling a little gutsy, try a level three for fun. You just might surprise yourself. And you might try challenging another player, double or nothing, winner take all. You pick the difficulty level. If he gets it right, he takes double points, you lose double points. You could probably even devise a handicap system if you really want to be fair about it, however that might be moving just a little too close to the brink of insanity.

Anyhow, I would suggest keeping some sort of tally going. It's how we separate the real fanatics from the wannabes. I've run across a lot of people who claim to know *everything* about *The Brady Bunch*, but by the time I'm through with them, they wish they'd never even heard of the Bradys.

The last thing I want you to keep in mind is *use the Episode Guide*! If you don't remember the scenario in which the situation occurred, refer to the Episode Guide and refresh your memory. This can only help you answer future questions. And on the same note, why not study the Episode Guide prior to a Brady trivia show-down? I realize if you own this book, you probably already have a solid foundation of Brady knowledge, however, even *I* have a tendency to forget who did what to whom and why.

Have fun and good luck!

Just how many episodes are there, you may be asking yourself? One hundred and sixteen, plus the pilot.* And if you're reading this book, you've probably seen them all. Just how many times you've seen each episode is the real question. Me? This is only a guestimate, but I would have to say I have seen each episode, on average, at least . . . sixty times? Given the fact that it's been thirty years since the first episode aired, and I've seen each episode, on average, twice a year, if not more (I could be grossly underestimating), that makes sixty. And yes, I am taking into consideration all those Sunday afternoon Brady Bonanzas, Brady Marathons, Brady Getaways, Brady Star-Studded Weekends, Very Barrys, and Marcia Madness's. Although that would seem to take me way past the sixty-marker, as frenetic as I am about watching *The Brady Bunch*, I do have a life, you know.

In the back of the book is a numerical list of the episodes as well as a brief synopsis of each (including the subplot, if there is one). Should the title of the episode not be enough to jog your memory, feel free to use the Episode Guide. Now, if this doesn't clarify things for you, I would suggest putting this book away and brushing up a bit more before you go any further. Watch a few more episodes. You're obviously not ready for this caliber of trivia. Besides, you won't have the pleasure of racking your brains if you have to look up everything.

---

* This number does not include the subsequent Brady permutations, *The Brady Kids, The Brady Bunch Variety Hour, The Brady Girls Get Married (a.k.a. The Brady Brides), A Very Brady Christmas, The Bradys, The Brady Bunch Movie,* or *A Very Brady Sequel,* nor will any of my questions reflect these mutant revivals as my *Brady Bunch* knowledge is limited to the original series (as well as my loyalty).

Part Two

The Questions

1 For whom did Alice keep house before Mike and Carol were married?

2 What letter was Carol referring to when she said, "And you thought this letter was about us?"

3 What was Peter referring to when he asked Carol, "Then how do you explain all the awful things that have been happening to us since we found it?"

4 Who was Kitty KarryAll?

5 Which Brady was allergic to flea powder?

6 Which Brady child snuck out of the bedroom window in the middle of the night to mail a letter?

7 Who asked Bobby, "As long as I'm here, why don't we throw a few passes together?"

8 What landed on Rachel's head while she and Greg were at a drive-in movie?

9 Mike: "That solved the whole problem, Ed. The kids have their _____ in the family room. I have *mine* in here in my den."

10 Where were Bobby and Cindy when Cindy said, "It's all your fault. You wanted to chase after that Indian boy"?

11 Who was Marcia referring to when she said, "That's what I was trying to tell you. We're running *against* each other"?

12 Which Bradys were held captive in an ancient burial ground in Hawaii?

13 What was the hobby of Marcia's very first steady boyfriend, Harvey Klinger?

14 How did Marcia combat her fear and pass her driver's test?

15 What was the Brady dog's name?

16 Who asked, "Can I really call you Desi?"

17 Which Brady met his/her double?

18 To whom did Buddy Hinton say, "Baby talk, baby talk, it's a wonder you can walk!"?

19 Which Brady girl decided to go brunette?

20 Which Brady reluctantly played the part of Benedict Arnold in the school play about George Washington?

21 Which Brady boy saved Peter from a falling ladder?

22 What was Millicent referring to when she told Bobby, "You shouldn't have done that. I'm contagious. The doctor thinks I may have the mumps!"?

23 Marcia: "Hey Mom. I was thinking. Once the _____ gets cleaned out, it would make a great extra room."

24 Which Brady girl borrowed Carol's favorite earrings without asking, then lost them?

25 Which Brady boy said, "You know, it *could* be. Well, this may sound ridiculous, but it's just *possible* that Jennifer was trying to use me to win that cheerleading contest"?

26 Who said, "Myron wasn't exterminated! He's in the hamper upstairs in our room!"?

27 Who said, "My beautiful little locket, gone, as mysteriously as it came"?

28 What color was Alice's uniform?

29 What did Mike do for a living?

30 Who stepped on the Chinese Checkers game, slipped and fell, and sprained an ankle?

31 Which Brady fell in love with the new family dentist?

32 Who said, "I'm going to prove you and Mom were right for trusting me. I'm going to find out how those cigarettes got there"?

33 Which Brady girl so closely resembled Carol's Aunt Jenny as a child?

34 What color were the bedspreads in the boys' room?

35 Who designed the Brady house?

36 To whom did Carol say, "Well, you'll still have to go along with your punishment at school, but the slumber party is on again!"?

37 Who said, "I've joined the Science Club at school and I'm building a volcano. And when I'm finished I can make it erupt"?

38 Who was Carol referring to when she said, "He couldn't have looked back because *I* was moving first!"?

39 Who did Marcia want to sing at her prom?

40 Why did Jan pull down all of Marcia's awards and hide them in the closet?

41 Which Brady said, "Being in the middle is like being invisible"?

42 Which Brady boy said, "That's what I'll do. I'll pick an instrument tomorrow"?

43 Whose horoscope read, "A strange woman will soon come into your life"?

44 What color was the kitchen table?

45 What was Mike referring to when he told Bobby and Peter, "Well, if it shows up again, ask Flash Brady here. She'll take some pictures of it for you"?

46 With whom did a falsely mustached Peter go on a double date?

47 Who did Marcia and Jan try to set up with Great Grandma Hutchins?

48 What famous bank robber did Bobby idolize?

49 Who was Marcia referring to when she said, "One of the mothers and her daughter are going to do a duet"?

50 Who said, "I'm just going to have to say, 'Dad, I don't like it. I'm no good at it. I don't want to be an architect'"?

51 Which Brady had a column in the school paper?

52 Against whom did Bobby compete in a chin-up contest?

53 Which Brady boy was reluctant to ask Carol if he could join the football team at school?

54 What kind of commercial were the Bradys asked to make?

55 Who showed up at the Brady house as Alice was getting ready for her date with Mark Millard, her old high school flame?

56 Who said, "Now everybody's got a trophy . . . except me"?

57 What was Greg referring to when he said, "I'm in the Pony League"?

58 Peter to Cousin Oliver: "Hey Oliver, you moved in at a great time! We're going on a tour of a _____ Saturday!"

59 What was Kathy Kelly, the Brady's new neighbor, referring to when she told Carol, "I can hardly wait for Monday when I take those three to school to register them. What an assortment!"?

60 What did Peter mean when he told Marcia, "And when Westdale finds out that *my* sister's a double agent, they might not even let me in!"?

61 Who was Greg referring to when he said, "I guess she figures because I'm the oldest, I must be the leader"?

62 What did the Brady kids all chip in for, for Mike and Carol's anniversary?

63 Who said, "When the teacher asked for a volunteer, not one kid in the class raised his hand. Not one kid. So she made me the safety monitor. The class cop"?

64 What did Alice's cousin Emma, who came to stay with the Bradys while Alice was on vacation, do for a living?

65 Which Brady boy was convinced he was dull?

66 Who was the first Brady child to receive his/her driver's license?

67 What was Carol referring to when she said, "Mike, you're a park wrecker"?

68 Which Brady girl said, "I want to join the Frontier Scouts"?

69 What was Carol referring to when she said, "No one is going to read this article until I'm finished!"?

70 Who made a movie about the pilgrims for a history class assignment?

71 Which Brady saved a little girl's life at the local toy store?

72 What medical ailment did all the Brady kids come down with at once?

73 Who was Alice referring to when she said, "He's two hundred pounds of unbudgeable bachelor and anything else is trivia"?

74 Which Brady snuck a goat into the house in the middle of the night?

75 To whom did Mike say, "I think you'd better spend some time thinking about your driving habits while you don't use the car for a week"?

76 Who said, "I wish I were an only child!"?

77 Which Brady girl was nominated hostess for Senior Banquet Night?

78 Who said, "Baby?! Why did I have to be born so young?"

79 Who said, "I've been up in my room all afternoon working on this sure-fire hit song"?

80 Which Brady secretly taped the other Bradys' private conversations?

81 Where did the Bradys stop on their way to the Grand Canyon?

82 Who was Greg referring to when he said, "And I was the editor of the yearbook, a member of student council for three semesters, and I've had a lot more experience than my worthy opponent"?

83 What was the predominant color of the furniture in the boy's room?

84 Who said, "I wouldn't kiss a girl for nothin'!"?

85 Which Brady brought a mouse home for a school science project?

86 Which Brady lay in bed saying, "You know something? It's hard to talk with your mouth full of toothpaste!"?

87 Who said, "Tomorrow's graduation and I've got . . . orange hair!"?

88 What picture was Bobby referring to when he said, "Gee, that's swell. I really like this picture but I didn't want to upset my new mom"?

89 Who said, "Spending the afternoon with three girls isn't as easy as I thought it would be"?

90 Who said, "Seven silver swans swam silently seaward"?

91 Where was Alice's bedroom located?

92 Which Brady worked part-time for Mike?

93 To whom did Cindy say, "If you steal one more thing Daddy's going to send you to Siberia!"?

94 What happened when Mike and Carol checked up on the kids the first time they left them home alone?

95 Mike to Carol: "Emergency or no emergency, those kids can't use my _____!"

96 Which Brady kid sold hair tonic door to door?

97 Who told Cousin Oliver, "I've got an idea. All the other kids left for school. Now you stand guard and I'll see if Marcia wrote about me in her diary"?

98 Mike to the family: "The plans are for a big _____, and I thought you'd all like to go with me!"

99 Which Brady volunteered the entire family to put on the play *Snow White and the Seven Dwarfs?*

100 Which Brady was played by Maureen McCormick?

101 Who sculpted Mike's head for an art competition?

102 Who said, "She always says, 'Don't play ball in the house'"?

103 Which Bradys slept in bunk beds?

104 Which Brady boy was a Frontier Scout?

105 Why was it so important that Carol regain her voice by Christmas day?

106 Who was supposed to be locked up in Mike's car during his and Carol's wedding?

107 Who wrote the winning jingle for the Ever Pressed Fabric Company jingle contest?

108 Who said, "Oh, come on, Alice. You know I couldn't go without my best girl. It just wouldn't be any fun"?

109 Which Brady was played by Susan Olson?

110 What was Marcia planning when she said, "Let's see, I've already invited Jenny Wilton, my best friend, and Paula Tardy from my English class"?

111 To whom did Mike say, "You're going to be making deliveries on your bicycle. Blueprints, drawings, revisions. And that carries with it a great deal of responsibility"?

112 Who was Dr. Howard referring to when he said, "Well, she's running a low fever and her tonsils are quite inflamed. We've been through this before, Mr. Brady. They really should come out"?

113 What did Jan buy to change her image?

114 Which Brady boy had a crush on his math teacher?

115 What was Alice's boyfriend's name?

116 What kind of speech impediment did Cindy have?

117 To whom did Cindy say, "You look beautiful. But how *do* you get the toothpaste through all that barbed wire?"

118 Which Brady was played by Eve Plumb?

119 Which Bradys had the measles at the same time?

120 What tropical paradise did Mike's boss send the entire family to?

121 Which Brady child was accused of stealing another child's bike at the school playground?

122 Who was Alice referring to when she said, "This is just a little something for Mr. Teeter and Miss Totter"?

123 Which Brady was afraid of the dark in one particular episode?

124 Which Brady became afraid of heights after falling from a tree?

125 What was Greg referring to when he said, "It's full of tens and twenties and fifties"?

126 Who wrote in her diary, "My dream of dreams is to be Mrs. Desi Arnaz Jr."?

127 What was Mike referring to when he said, "Would you change the amount of the reward, please, from $37.26 to $42.76?"

128 Who was Cindy referring to when she yelled, "He took my doll!"?

129 Who said, "You don't work for a man all these years and not know what kind of a man he is!"?

130 Who said, "Who would send me a pool table?"

131 Which Brady girl was voted "Most Popular Girl"?

132 Which Brady yelled, "Peter Brady, you're fired!"?

133 To whom did Alice say, "You're always late, your prices are too high, and *that* is the ugliest necktie I ever saw!"?

134 Who was Carol referring to when she said, "My son, the bike doctor!"?

135 To whom did Carol say, "You're like a member of our family. We all love you very much"?

136 To whom did Greg say, "You pee-wees. You're always trying to act bigger than you are"?

137 What leading role did Marcia win in the school play?

138 What was Mike referring to when he said, "The question is, who broke it and who glued it together?"

139 What instrument did Greg play?

140 Why did Mike say, "It's hard to believe that was once my room"?

141 Why did Carol tell Cindy, "And then when you wake up, you can have all the ice cream you want"?

142 Which Brady was played by Mike Lookinland?

143 Who was Mike referring to when he said, "Well, she's been rehearsing her solo day and night for the church service Christmas morning"?

144 Who suggested, "If you're both so sure you're right, next Saturday, why don't you simply switch jobs?"

145 Who said, "It's like I said. It's my aunt in Sacramento"?

146 What made Mike and Carol's honeymoon different than most honeymoons?

147 Who said, "I'd rather kiss a basketball and a catcher's mitt than any dumb girl"?

148 Who said, "Holy Mackerel! You look just like me!"?

149 What was Harvey Klinger referring to when he told Marcia, "It's an absolute perfect specimen!"?

150 What board game did we see the Brady children enjoy more than any other game?

151 What was Greg referring to when he told Marcia, "Look, I know how you feel and I can't blame you. But I honestly think Mom and Dad made the fair decision"?

152 Why did Cindy say, "I don't want Greg or Marcia blowing my nose. I can do it myself"?

153 Who doodled the doodle, entitled "Mrs. Denton: A Hippopotamus"?

154 Who told Greg, "Men! You all want your women to look beautiful but you're unwilling to cooperate!"?

155 Which Brady was played by Christopher Knight?

156 Who said, "I think I'll send Aunt Jenny a picture of myself"?

157 Who said, "They said I talk funny. They said I talk like a baby"?

158 How did Peter try to get over his fear of talking to Kerry Hathaway, Jan's pretty, new friend?

159 Who said, "Now that I won't tattle anymore, will you tell me some secrets?"

160 Who said, "He's better than a doctor, he's Santa Claus!"?

161 Who helped Cindy try to find Carol's favorite earrings, which she lost after borrowing them without asking?

162 What was Greg referring to when he said, "Say, if Marcia isn't mad, maybe Jennifer won't be mad either. After all, Jennifer's crazy about me!"?

163 Which Brady faked sickness on his/her first day of high school?

164 To whom did Cindy say, "We didn't see you look back . . . just like the man said"?

165 What caused all the commotion at Mike and Carol's wedding?

166 Who was Cindy talking to when she said, "You're lucky, on account of having *my* mother for your stepmother"?

167 Which Brady spoke out on the local news about Women's Lib?

168 Who said, "Fighting's dumb, Buddy. Let's try reasoning together"?

169 To whom did Mike say, "There is something you should be thinking about—all the problems you could have caused by hiding the fact that you'd been exposed to the mumps"?

170 Who was Marcia referring to when she said, "I'll go right over to his hotel and ask him"?

171 Who said, "Finally, I did it. Something Marcia's never done in her whole life"?

172 Who said, "I'm looking for a wig"?

173 Why did Peter's football teammates call him a canary?

174 Who said, "He asked me to go steady with him! I said yes if you said yes! Can I Mom, please?"

175 Which Brady was played by Robert Reed?

176 Who said to Mike, "Ah ha! Then a strange woman *did* enter your life today!"?

177 Why did Cindy say, "I get to fly and marry a prince and everything!"?

178 What side of the bed did Carol sleep on (from the viewer's perspective)?

179 Who said, "You'd think I could find *one* guy willing to go out on a blind date"?

180 What other character besides Mike Brady did Robert Reed play in *The Brady Bunch*?

181 Who said, "Whoever heard of a mean stepfather? It's only the mother who's famous for mean"?

182 Who said, "We've got a household of children and women who are scared to death of mice . . . particularly the one who's talking to you"?

183 Who said, "Playing ball with three boys wasn't exactly a breeze either"?

184 Who wrote a paper for school that read, "He was a great American and his name was Jesse James"?

185 With whom did Marcia do a song and dance from the musical *Gypsy* at the Westdale High's Family Night Frolics?

186 Who told Marcia, "If only Dad hadn't given me these beautiful tools. Now he expects me to draw something terrific"?

187 Which Brady was known as "Scoop Brady" in one particular episode?

188 What was Greg referring to when he told Carol, "*That's* not from practice. I did that when I bumped my arm in math class"?

189 What kind of pet did the Brady family own in the earlier episodes?

190 What did Bobby see when kissed by Millicent?

191 Why did Mike and Carol go home in the middle of their wedding night?

192 Who said, "If any of my boys wanted to play in anybody's doll house, I'd take them to a psychiatrist!"?

193 Who said, "Chopping and tracking is nice, I guess, if you're a boy. It really is. I just wanted to prove to myself I could do it, even if I'm a girl"?

194 Which Brady child tried smoking and got caught?

195 Who said, "Sam's idea of romance is two pounds of liver . . . heart-shaped!"?

196 Which Brady was played by Barry Williams?

197 Why did Carol say, "Well, kids, I never thought I'd say this to you, but I want you to go outside and . . . get dirty!"?

198 Who was Mike referring to when he told Alice, "He's an incurable gambler. Horses, cards, you name it"?

199 Which Brady said, "I just gotta get a trophy. I just gotta"?

200 To whom did Buddy Hinton give a black eye?

201 Who was Carol referring to when she said, "He eats and sleeps baseball"?

202 What was Marcia referring to when she told the man at the store, "We won, 'cause everything counts when you're building a house"?

203 Who was Carol referring to when she said, "She hasn't sneezed a single sneeze"?

204 Who was Mike referring to when he said, "Well, the kids are giving him a warm welcome"?

205 Greg: "Now all I have to do is give this phony _____ to Marcia and have her invite Jerry over tomorrow"?

206 Which Brady was told, "You are a superstar! You are the new Johnny Bravo!"?

207 Which Brady was played by Florence Henderson?

208 Who was Bobby referring to when he told Mike, "You said if we didn't find him, you would put a lost and found ad in the paper"?

209 Which Bradys had their tonsils out at the same time?

210 Why was Greg failing his math class in one particular episode?

211 Why did Cindy say to Jan, "The top of your hair turned black!"?

212 What was Jan referring to when she said, "And I came in the next day and ordered the engraving . . . is it ready?"

213 What was Marcia referring to when she said, "Well, I guess if you're lucky enough, you could find one anywhere. Maybe even in a dentist's office"?

214 Who was Cindy referring to when she told Carol, "He stopped seven kids from running down the stairs. And he was still trying to get their names when I left"?

215 What was Carol referring to when she told Mike, "How could I forget?! Alice is coming home! The prisoners of war are about to be liberated!"?

216 What was Mike referring to when he told Carol, "Look, he's only got a hundred bucks. He's not going to be satisfied with anything he could get for that"?

217 What did the city hall want to tear down in order to build a new county courthouse?

218 What was Carol referring to when she told Alice, "As a matter of fact, you're here at a very special time! Just two more words. 'The End'"?

219 Why did the entire Brady family dress up as pilgrims and Indians?

220 Who did Ann B. Davis play?

221 What was Marcia referring to when she told Mike, "It was the only place I could find that was private. I'm sorry if I made you angry"?

222 To whom did Bobby say, "He wants Sam to get the plans away from my dad!"?

223 Which Brady girl said, "I took your advice Mom. I took up tap dancing"?

224 What was Greg referring to when he said, "There was no place else to hide her till after the game tonight"?

225 Who was Cindy referring to when she told Bobby, "I wrote him a letter and I signed your name to it. So he's coming here this afternoon"?

226 To whom did Mike say, "Your mother and I believe that you knew precisely what we meant. But if you want to live by exact words, okay"?

227 What was Bobby referring to when he said, "We can't wait to see Miss Smarty Pants [Cindy] fall right on her big, fat head"?

228 To whom did Peter say, "You just lost yourself five brothers and sisters!"?

229 What was Marcia's dilemma after being nominated for hostess for Senior Banquet Night?

230 Who said, "I'll show them! From now on, I'm gonna be an older woman!"?

231 What was Greg referring to when he said, "Look at the title! 'We Can Make the World a Whole Lot Brighter' "?

232 Who said, "I kind of bugged the rooms with Dad's tape recorder"?

233 Where were the Bradys on their way to when they stopped to spend the night at an old deserted ghost town?

234 Why did Jan rub lemons on her face?

235 To whom did Cindy say, "She isn't here and I can't tell you anything else 'cause I'm not a tattletale anymore"?

236 Who told Bobby, "Never open the front door without asking who it is"?

237 What was Jan referring to when she said, "I've worn it to bed every night since I got it"?

238 Mike: "Those kids are using that _____ constantly and we have *got* to do something drastic."

239 Who said, "I'll handle the really big decisions, like how much butter on the toast, how long to bake the potatoes, that sort of thing. But when it comes to trivia, like how to salvage a family . . . "?

240 What was the significance of, "I talked to that talent scout again. The studio people loved the photo of Cindy I submitted"?

241 Marcia to Greg: "I'll bet you I get a higher score on my _____ than you got."

242 Which Brady was hit in the nose by a football?

243 Who was Marcia referring to when she said, "You lost the bet. You didn't stay up there all night"?

244 Why did Mike's boss send him and the family to Hawaii?

245 Which Brady girl wore glasses?

246 What was Bobby referring to when he said, "We've been going at it since three minutes after eight this morning"?

247 Who said, "I can't sleep with the light off!"?

248 Who told Mike, "They want me to play a gig with them at Stephen Decatur High. Isn't that a gas?"

249 Which Brady sprained his/her ankle climbing a tree?

250 What was Mike referring to when he said, "I'm going to turn it over to the police"?

251 Where was Marcia's diary mistakenly donated to?

252 Why was Alice laid up in bed in one particular episode?

253 What was Greg referring to when he told Bobby, "Maybe Cindy was right. Maybe you *did* take it after all"?

254 Which Brady dreamed of becoming a world champion pool player?

255 To whom did Mike say, "You promised them everything in the world for getting elected and you gave nothing in return"?

256 To whom did Marcia say, "I fired you because you're lazy and you deserved it!"?

257 Who said, "Mr. Martinelli says I'm not mechanically inclined"?

258 Who was Greg referring to when he told Carol, "Well, we never wanted her to leave"?

259 To whom did Sam say, "What do you say, Shrimpo?"

260 Who was Carol referring to when she said, "She got the part of Juliet"?

261 Which Brady asked to stay behind from the annual camping trip?

262 Dr. Howard: "Mrs. Brady, your _____ are as bad as Cindy's."

263 What was Mr. Randolph, the school principal, referring to when he told Marcia, "Mrs. Denton found this when she was tidying up the desks in her room"?

264 Who said, "Hold it! Marcia, look! No organization. See, *that's* the trouble with women. You should only go to the refrigerator once and take out everything you need. Look, I'll show you"?

265 Who was Carol referring to when she said, "She made the whole thing up because she thinks we don't need her"?

266 To whom did Alice say, "I'm sure you are going to be very happy. Mrs. Martin is a lovely woman"?

267 Peter to Arthur Owens: "Holy Mackerel, you look just like _____!"

268 To whom did Bobby say, "It's nice to know that you think I'm so brave, but honest . . . "?

269 Why did Bobby say, "I guess I'll just have to stay away from everybody till tomorrow morning"?

270 Who told Jan, "I wrote Kerry a letter, and I slipped it into her locker. I want to know what she said about it"?

271 Who was Mike referring to when he said, "She's just so uptight about high school, she's come down with some imaginary symptoms"?

272 What was Mike referring to when he said, "How could four of you have been in the car and two of you see one thing and two of you see another?"

273 Who said, "That's one thing my sister's never done, is been a pompom girl"?

274 Name one of the three Bradys who sang in the school Glee Club?

275 Who said, "No, darling, fluffier, fluffier! My factory has to be fluffier!"?

276 Who said, "Please, Daddy. Please don't interrupt my 'hersal"?

277 What side of the bed did Mike sleep on (from the viewer's perspective)?

278 Captain McCartney: "I'm here to investigate an alleged sighting of an alleged _____."

279 What was Greg referring to when he told Peter, "Don't say too much. Be the strong, silent type. That way you can't make too many mistakes"?

280 What other character besides Carol Brady did Florence Henderson play on *The Brady Bunch*?

281 What beverage do we see Mike and Carol enjoying most often?

282 Who told Greg, "I took him out of his cage in your room last night, just to play a joke"?

283 Who said, "If after all this, I were to come up with something weirder, he'd have to admit I'd starve as an architect"?

284 Who asked Greg, "How come you take such good pictures and I take such rotten ones?"

285 What was Carol referring to when she told Mike, "You're just in time for the judging. On the left is Pile A and on the right is Pile B"?

286 Who was Carol referring to when she said, "And he uses unsuspecting women to support himself"?

287 Which Brady entered an ice cream eating contest?

288 Who told Peter, "I've been practicing. Now I can speak really swell!"?

289 How did Peter break Carol's favorite vase?

290 Who said, "I'm going to be a baseball player. They don't have to know anything"?

291 Who said, "I'll bet you a million dollars you can't do twice as many chin-ups as I can"?

292 What was the grand prize for being the one-millionth person to walk through Marathon Studio's gates?

293 Who did Jerry Rogers use in order to steal Greg's football playbook?

294 Mike to Carol: "In my mind, there was just never any question about _____ going to college."

295 What was the problem with the silver platter the kids bought for Mike and Carol's anniversary?

296 Who was Marcia referring to when she told Jan, "There's only one problem. To him I'm just a mouth full of teeth"?

297 To whom did Carol say, "Your father and I have just had a little talk. Now we don't know exactly what happened at school, but we think there has been a mistake. We believe what you said about the picture"?

298 What did Peter do for his first part-time job?

299 To whom did Marcia say, "I snitched to the folks about you smoking"?

300 Who said, "Watch it! I can also cite you for arguing with a safety monitor!"?

301 Who said, "Mirror, mirror on the wall, who's the dullest one of all?"

302 What was Greg's friend Eddie referring to when he said, "I'm only selling her because I need a fast hundred bucks"?

303 What was Mike's dilemma after the Brady family went on an all-out campaign to save Woodland Park?

304 Who said, "Mr. Delafield liked my story! He's going to buy it!"?

305 Where did Greg shoot his movie entitled *Our Pilgrim Fathers: Through Hardship to Freedom*?

306 Which Brady boy had a feature story written about him (including a photo)?

307 Who said, "A wise man forgets his anger before he lies down to sleep"?

308 Why did Bobby and Cousin Oliver lock Sam and his landlord in Sam's meat locker?

309 Who said, "You're right. I have no talent for tap dancing. In fact, I have no talent for anything at all"?

310 Who was Mike referring to when he told Carol, "I don't think we're letting him get away with anything because exact words are *pretty* hard to live by"?

311 Who assured Peter, "*My* stuff is even better than Cyrano's"?

312 Who said, "I want to be a teenager now!"?

313 What did the Brady kids call themselves when they recorded their first song?

314 Where did Zacchariah T. Brown hold the Bradys hostage before driving off in their car to stake his claim?

315 Which Brady girl said, "His name? It's George! George . . . uh . . . George . . . Glass. George Glass!"?

316 Mike to Jan: "When you get up in front of those VIPs, you picture them sitting there in their _____."

317 What was Cindy referring to when she said, "I thought I told him *this* Saturday. But I guess I made a mistake. We can't have the theater, it's rented!"?

318 Why did Marcia scream, "Oh, my nose!"?

319 What celebrity did Bobby and Cindy meet in Hawaii?

320 Who said, "What a dumbhead I am. How could I have taken someone else's bicycle?"

321 What was Art Winters of the *Daily Chronicle* referring to when he asked Bobby and Cindy, "How long have you kids been at it?"

322 Who was Greg referring to when he said, "I've got a date with a new girl and I don't want the All-American kid tagging along"?

323 Who said, "I only took a few puffs"?

324 Which Brady boy screamed, "Tiger, stop scaring my parakeet!"?

325 What did Marcia keep hidden in the garage in the earlier episodes?

326 Who was Marcia referring to when she told Greg, "I'll be the DA, 'cause everyone knows he's guilty"?

327 Which Brady beat everybody at pool?

328 Why were all of Jan's classmates angry with her after she was elected "Most Popular Girl"?

Part II

To whom did Sam say, "For your information, bowling balls are out this season and electric mixers are in"?

330 Who waited tables at the Golden Spoon Diner for a short while?

331 Marcia to Jan and Cindy: "Poor _____. He keeps measuring himself all the time."

332 How did Jan happen to ride her bike into the family portrait that was hidden out in the garage?

333 Who told the rest of the kids, "Guess what? I'm going to have a party tomorrow after school and you're all invited!"?

334 Who was Alice referring to when she told Carol, "I'll bet his voice was cracking then, too"?

335 Mike to Greg and Marcia: "Anyone who knocks the _____ off the pylon is a loser."

336 What celebrity played Bobby's ukulele in Hawaii?

337 Who was Peter's assistant in his magic show at school?

338 Who did Bobby find out *really* took his kazoo after blaming it on Cindy?

339 Who was Greg referring to when he said, "I have to teach him to run that maze by Monday"?

340 Who asked, "Dad, did you ever kiss a girl when you were my age?"

341 Who said, "Juliet? But I tried out for the part of the nurse"?

342 Who was Carol referring to when she said, "First he outgrows his family, then he wants his own room"?

343 What was Alice referring to when she told Carol, "When you get back, the ice cream will be ready and waiting"?

344 Who did Mike take to the mall to visit Santa Claus on Christmas Eve?

345 Which Brady child got locked in the bedroom closet?

346 To whom did Greg say, "I didn't mean to make you cry. I didn't know how much the room meant to you"?

347 What favorite item of Carol's was mangled in the washing machine?

348 What was Greg's dilemma when he was selected chairman of the committee to pick the head cheerleader?

349 Who said to Mike and Carol, "I was joining anything and everything, just to be popular"?

350 Who said, "Then Bobby and I will have to go to court. And the judge swears at you!"?

351 Who told Marcia, "That's the album my manager promised you"?

352 Which Brady thought he/she had won the school essay on Americanism, but in the end, came in second?

353 What kind of wig did Jan wear in order to be noticed?

354 To whom did Mike say, "If you want to give up the drums, it's perfectly all right with us"?

355 Who said, "Eenie, Meenie, Mommy, Daddy"?

356 To whom did Peter say, "I don't trust you. You stole my girl"?

357 What happened to ruin the chance for the Brady kids to record Greg's song, "We Can Make the World a Whole Lot Brighter"?

358 What was old Mr. Hanalei referring to when he told the boys, "Evil comes to those who touch"?

359 Who told Peter, "I'm ready, Peter the Great. So you can make me disappear now"?

360 Who told Marcia, "That's one of the nice things about being in show business . . . an occasional mention in a diary"?

361 Where was Peter when a big, hairy spider crawled across his chest?

362 Why did Mike say, "How about that? My den is funky"?

363 Which Bradys were amateur photographers?

364 What was Mike referring to when he said, "That walking lump of hair has an intangible something"?

365 Who sent Jan the mysterious little locket?

366 On what occasion did Mike say to Carol, "You, my dear, are prettier than a flower, sweeter than the cake, more appetizing than the hors d'oeuvres, and more sparkling than the silverware"?

367 What was Bobby referring to when he said, "I bought each bottle for a dollar. And the Neat & Natural Company guarantees I can sell each one for two dollars"?

368 Who was out of town when Alice fell and sprained her ankle?

369 Who played Alice's cousin Emma?

370 Who was Marcia referring to when she said, "My opponent has a lot more experience than I do in school government. Besides, I think he's real groovy"?

371 To whom did Carol say, "Next Saturday, Daddy is going to help you with your cooking badge"?

372 Who was Jan referring to when she said, "I'm going to write her right away. I can't wait to find out what she looks like!"?

373 What did Alice's boyfriend do for a living?

374 To whom did Greg say, "She said you could do a dramatic reading and I could accompany you on the guitar"?

375 To whom did Cindy say on the telephone, "I got your flowers and candy and big diamond ring"?

376 What was Carol referring to when she said, "Do you think we might get a chance to rehearse the script?"

377 Who was a contestant on *The Cartoon King Show*?

378 What was Greg referring to when he told Mike, "I'm never going to play that dumb game again"?

379 Who told Mike and Carol, "I feel like right now I've got to give a singing career a chance"?

380 Which Brady kids tried to borrow money from a bank?

381 Who was the married man Marcia fell in love with?

382 Who told a little girl, "We can't go in that old house. There's a sign right out in the front that says, NO TRESPASSING"?

383 Why did Alice's cousin Emma get the Brady family out of bed at 6 A.M.?

384 Where did Greg take his date, Rachel, when Bobby had to tag along?

385 Which Brady threw him/herself a party for being a hero?

386 Which Brady boy's voice changed throughout a particular episode?

387 Who said, "It's called family cooperation, boys. You scratch their backs and they'll scratch yours."

388 Who told Marcia, "I'll tell you why I'm here. I'm here to meet my number one fan"?

389 What was Cindy referring to when she said, "I'm sorry, but it's not my Kitty"?

390 Which Brady boy walked around acting like Humphrey Bogart in an attempt to change his personality?

391 What was Greg referring to when he said, "I had the hundred bucks in my hot little hands and then . . . I let the sucker off the hook"?

392 Who said, "Yeah, but you're just an ordinary spy. I'm a double agent"?

393 Who tried out for a part in the school play and wound up being discovered as a painter?

394 To whom did Mr. Berkley, the boys' vice principal, say, "And as for you, young man, I think a 5,000 word essay on mascot stealing is in order"?

395 Who was Mike referring to when he said, "Well, we can't *make* her stay. Abraham Lincoln put a stop to that"?

396 Mike: "Next Saturday morning, instead of me, _____ is going to help you with baseball practice."

397 Which Brady suffered from stage fright while appearing on TV?

398 Who said, "I'm not really grown up. I was just pretending, for a date!"?

399 Who said, "I *am* a lady! If you say I'm not, I'll bop you!"?

400 Which Brady girl was described by Clark Tyson as a tomboy?

401 What happened when Mike tried to make an important business call on the kids' pay phone?

402 Why did the Brady kids want to cancel their first Christmas together?

403 At what event did Carol scream, "Alice, can't you control that dog?!"

404 Why did Bobby run around the backyard screaming, "I won! I won! I won! I won!" while the rest of the family stood around him?

405 Why did Marcia fail her first driver's test?

406 Who said, "Cinderella's stepmother was real mean. I saw it on television with my own eyes"?

407 Who said, "Of all the crummy times for my voice to change"?

408 What was the man at the toy store referring to when he told Bobby, "She's sure lucky to have a brother like you"?

409 Who told Mike, "I'm in high school now. And when you're in high school, you're not a kid anymore"?

410 What did the Bradys run all over King's Island amusement park looking for?

411 Who said, "I broke my date with Charlie for the same night, just so I could go out with Doug Simpson"?

412 Who was Greg referring to when he told the other kids, "I'll bet if she saw something scary, she'd break the record for the mile run!"?

413 What was Mrs. Johnson referring to when she said, "Mrs. Brady, I can understand your wanting to believe your own son. If parents refuse to open their eyes, you are doing exactly what our committee is trying to prevent"?

414 What type of gymnastic equipment did Mike bring home in an effort to help Bobby with his fear of heights?

415 Why did Mr. Stoner come to the Brady house to see the boys?

416 Who said, "We're engaged"?

417 What was Mike referring to when he told Peter, "You should have told us, you know. Hiding out in the park hasn't helped anyone"?

418 Who said, "You see, my Uncle Winston has this very nice dress shop. The woman who runs it for him up and eloped"?

419 Who said, "Gee, I never thought I'd ever wish I was little!"?

420 What play was Marcia referring to when she said, "Mom, do you think they'd let me do it? I'll learn the lines real fast, word for word. And I won't cause any trouble, I promise"?

421 What was Bobby referring to when he told Greg, "Well, it's a good thing you had it or you could have been drowned!"?

422 Who thought Carol had real butterflies in her stomach on her wedding day?

423 Who said, "I don't want to spoil your great song, Greg"?

424 What did Bobby mean when he told Cindy, "I was only playing a joke. Sorry I scared you"?

425 Who dressed up in a black wig and dark glasses pretending to be Greg's girlfriend, Debbie, in an attempt to get Kerry Hathaway to dump him?

426 What was Bobby referring to when he told Cindy, "And I'm not giving this to you because I like you or anything like that. It's just that . . . well . . . my piggy bank was gettin' too full and I had to buy something"?

427 Where was Alice when she said, "It's my hula, Mrs. Brady. My *hu* went one way and my *la* went the other"?

428 To whom did Arthur Owens say, "And you look just like me without glasses!"?

429 Which Brady girl tried out for the head cheerleading contest with Greg on the panel of judges?

430 Who told Mike and Carol, "The Boosters are *the* most popular club. And they only take in three freshman a year and I'll know tomorrow if they'll accept me"?

431 Who said, "He didn't even look back. He just barreled right out of that parking slot!"?

432 Who guest-starred on *The Brady Bunch* as himself and sang a song entitled "Girl"?

433 Who was Deacon Jones referring to when he said, "You think this guy can't play football 'cause he sings?"

434 Who told Alice, "You're their *step*-housekeeper. And nobody like steps as good as they like the real ones"?

435 Which Brady girl said, "But I *do* have a boyfriend. He's one of the nicest boys in school and he thinks I'm super cool"?

436 To whom did Cindy say, "Mommy's got larygitis *real* bad"?

437 Who said, "I always dream about bells . . . wedding bells . . . and then I wake up"?

438 The Brady family did a re-enactment of the events leading up to the disappearance of what?

439 Who said, "Hard work is an hour in the sun with three grow-ing boys"?

440 Why did Buddy Hinton tease Cindy?

441 Who said, "You think girls are more important than basket-ball?"

442 What kind of dog was Tiger?

443 Which Brady boy slept closest to the bathroom in the earlier episodes?

444 Who was *really* Cindy's secret admirer?

445 What was Mike referring to when he said, "Okay, let's go ahead with it. If Rome can outlast an invasion by the Barbarians, what can a few little girls do to the Brady house?"

446 Who took the boys fishing after Mike found out he had to work for Beebe Gallini, his cosmetic queen client, at the last minute?

447 Who asked Alice, "You mean I can only ask one person to the play?"

448 Why did Peter call himself "Phil Packer" in one particular episode?

449 What happened while Alice was taking a hula lesson in Hawaii?

450 What was Marcia describing when she said, "It's about this big, and it had a brown leather cover and I had it hidden behind the sleeping bags in the garage"?

451 What color was the Brady's station wagon?

452 What was Bobby referring to when he said, "I wouldn't do a thing like that. Maybe we fight sometimes, but Cindy's my sister. And, well, well, I just wouldn't do a thing like that"?

453 Why did Mike say to Bobby, "Next time you'll have to be more careful who you pick for a hero"?

454 Who said, "Yes, I do like to sing. But not in front of a bunch of mothers!"?

455 Who told Greg, "Every time I try and take a picture, everyone comes out lookin' dumb"?

456 Who was Mike referring to when he said, "He was so cocky, he wouldn't listen to the coach"?

457 To whom did Carol say, "You heard Jan sneezing just now? Well, she didn't sneeze once while you were at the office"?

458 To whom did Tami Cutler say, "Did anyone ever tell you that your profile would look great on an album cover?"

459 Alice: "_____ and I are in the semifinals of the mixed doubles tournament."

460 What was Greg's friend Eddie referring to when he told him, "You know, I've got five or six guys waiting to buy this baby"?

461 What was Mr. Phillips, Mike's boss, referring to when he said, "Mike, your family is jeopardizing our contract with the city"?

462 Who wrote, "And even though he's been my father a short time, no father could be a realer father than Michael Brady"?

463 Who said, "The play's about an American girl in Paris who's starving and painting and trying to pay her bills. And . . . while I'm telling you this, I should be learning my lines! I have to know them by tomorrow"?

464 To whom did Cindy say, "The letter I wrote him kind of gave him the idea that you were very, very sick"?

465 Why wasn't Cindy able to answer a single question on the *Question the Kids* television game show?

466 Who received a candy bar, wrapped in a note that read, "You don't know me, but I sure dig you. From, your secret admirer"?

467 Who was Mike referring to when he said, "Hey! He's taking the car and the trailer!"?

468 Why did the boys go to the ancient burial ground while in Hawaii?

469 Why did Mike decide to sell the house?

470 Marcia to Mike: "We don't want a _____. You can't lie on the floor and talk."

471 Who pranced down the stairs dressed like Shirley Temple?

472 What was Cindy referring to when she said, "I already told Mrs. Whitfield about the big day for her. And we ordered the books already. And now it's ruined and it's all my fault!"?

473 Who smashed Carol's sculpture of Mike to pieces?

474 Who said, "Mrs. Johnson's been after me to join her anti-smoking committee"?

475 Who said, "We never even shook hands. What made you think we got married?!"

476 Who said, "But this was my *first* job. And I bombed out, after only three days"?

477 Who was Carol referring to when she told Greg and Marcia, "I'm afraid sorry won't help. Sometimes when you push people too far, you just can't bring them back again!"?

478 Who was Bobby referring to when he said, "I think we should let him sing with us, even if he ruins everything"?

479 Why did the boys go to visit old Mr. Hanalei while in Hawaii?

480 Who told the deliveryman, "Mister, you keep calling me Sweetie, Cutie, and Gorgeous and I'll follow you anywhere"?

481 Who was Cindy referring to when she told Peter, "You made him disappear, just like that lady! And he's never coming back!"?

482 Who told Peter, "Jan's going to tell Kerry that nobody trusts me, that I'm a no-good, two-timing, double-crossing rat"?

483 Why did Carol ask Jan, "Where do you sit in Mrs. Denhoff's class?"

484 What was Cindy referring to when she told Carol, "Yes, but going down that rabbit hole is so exciting!"?

485 Who said, "A man doesn't want to be pestered by kids; he wants privacy. I think we have to make some changes around here"?

486 What was Carol referring to when she told Bobby after he had had a nightmare, "That talk with Mr. Collins really got through to you, huh?"

487 Who said, "If my customers don't buy one, I'll put my thumb on the scale!"?

488 Who said, "This is personal. Between my secret admirer and me"?

489 Why was Peter fired from his job at Mr. Martinelli's bike shop?

490 What was Peter referring to when he said, "G-g-g-get it off me! Please get it off me!"?

491 Who told Marcia, "I know his mother's housekeeper and she says that Desi Jr. is a real groovy kid"?

492 On what occasion did Carol say, "Oh, I forgot. Champagne has a terrible effect on me. It makes me dizzy"?

493 To whom did Greg say, "I'd like to see you prove you can do anything boys can do"?

494 Who suggested Mike and Carol switch roles for a day?

495 Who said, "I start working tomorrow, Randi. That car's getting closer by the minute"?

496 To whom did Greg say, "Did you ever try kissing a basketball?"

497 Who told Mike, "Hank's got his own apartment. And he's looking for someone to share the expenses"?

498 Why did Jan decide to go brunette?

499 Who said, "When you two promised to love, honor, etc., I promised to butt out"?

500 Who said, "I'd have to be twins. Hey! Did you hear what I just said?"

501 Who said, "Bobby, how can I enjoy a dumb old party knowing that the person who saved my life is sitting at home with a bad case of static?"

502 Who blurted out, "So that's why you did it! Even my own father knew I wouldn't be popular!"?

503 Why did Carol have to appear in court?

504 Who was Mike referring to when he said, "I guess every kid in town is trying to see him"?

505 Why did Peter say, "I might as well quit the Glee Club"?

506 To whom did Carol say, "It's somevun who calls me dahling and vants to speak to you"?

507 Peter: "*I'm* the guy who busted the _____."

508 Why did Alice sullenly explain to Peter, "Just an old family recipe that's been handed down from generation to generation . . . ending with this one"?

509 Who was Carol referring to when she said, "Oh, that's a *good* picture of him! And a feature story too!"?

510 To whom was Cindy referring when she told Carol, "You know how much we like him? This much!"?

511 Who said, "I wrote Kerry a letter and I slipped it into her locker. I want to know what she said about it"?

512 Marcia to Alan Anthony: "I don't believe you! You're lying! You just don't want to be seen with a girl who has _____!"

513 What relative, as a child, did Jan so closely resemble?

514 Who said, "What's happened is what I remembered. I completely forgot about The Little Bear"?

515 Carol to Marcia: "Well, you'll still have to go along with your punishment at school, but the _____ is on again!"?

516 What was Alice referring to when she said, "I saw that little pink nose twitching at me and I panicked!"?

517 Greg: "Tomorrow's graduation and I've got . . . _____!"

518 Bobby: "Say, that's right, Alice. You're my *real* housekeeper and you're only a _____ to them"?

519 Who said, "I chinned myself five times"?

520 Who was covered in layers of leis upon her arrival in Hawaii?

521 Which Brady thought he/she had a secret admirer?

522 What was Bobby's paper about Jesse James entitled?

523 What was Carol referring to when she said, "I'm sorry, kids, the invitation is just for the grown-ups"?

524 What was Marcia referring to when she said, "Not only did I pass, I got the highest score in the class"?

525 Why did Marcia lose the part of Juliet in the school play *Romeo and Juliet*?

526 Who was Bobby referring to when he said, "He always has dinner at our house whenever he's in town"?

527 What was Jan allergic to?

528 What was the name of Cindy's favorite doll?

529 Who said, "All my fiends are going to Tower High and I have to go to Westdale. Just because of this dumb street we live on"?

530 Why did Peter say, "I'll try harder, Mr. Martinelli"?

531 Where was Peter when he saved a little girl's life?

532 Why did Greg hole himself up in his bedroom, not letting anyone in?

533 How did Marcia bruise her nose?

534 To whom did Jan say, "Don't pretend you don't remember, after what you did yesterday while Clark and I were studying"?

535 What was Greg referring to when he told Marcia, "Four points less than I got"?

536 What contest was the journalist from the *Daily Chronicle* referring to when he said, "We've been conducting this contest for years and we have never read a tribute like that"?

537 Why did Tami Cutler tell Greg, "Do me a favor and call me at ten o'clock tomorrow morning"?

538 Why did Bobby yell, "Peter! Look out!"?

539 What was Carol referring to when she told Marcia, "But wouldn't you feel all alone up here by yourself?"

540 Where did Marcia keep her diary in which she wrote her fantasies about Desi Arnaz Jr.?

541 Greg: "You mean it, Dad? I can really have your _____?"

542 What was Mike referring to when he told Carol, "He also says he has an eyewitness who says she [Jan] stole it"?

543 Which two Bradys re-enacted *Cyrano De Bergerac*?

544 Who said, "It was something I saw at Jeremy's birthday party. The magician. He put a lady in a big box and made her disappear"?

545 To whom did Marcia say, "You told Mom that I left the record player on all night. Now I can't use the stereo for a whole week"?

546 Who did the Bradys mistakenly think was going to elope?

547 Who said to Jan, "Greg's smoking!"?

548 To whom did Cindy say, "I've got an idea. All the other kids left for school. Now you stand guard and I'll see if Marcia wrote about me in her diary"?

549 Who was Burt Grossman?

550 Who said, "I was picked out of all the kids at school to be on a television show!"?

551 For which Los Angeles Dodger did Mike design a house?

552 What was Carol referring to when she said, "Cindy, honey, don't you want to stay and watch Peter rehearse for his big tryout tomorrow?"

553 Who was Cindy referring to when she said, "Mommy, she cries black tears!"?

554 Where was Bobby when he asked Greg, "You mean we're locked in?"

555 Which two kids locked Sam and his landlord in Sam's meat locker?

556 Greg: "I won't tell anyone about your phone call to the sergeant if you don't tell anyone about my _____."

557 Why did Tiger run away?

558 What did Alice step on that caused her to slip and fall and sprain her ankle?

559 Carol: "Darling. Do you know what time it is? It's time to get a second _____. You've added three daughters and a wife to your household. That's four extra mouths."

560 Why did the Bradys build a dunk tank?

561 Who wrote, "Dear Soul Sister: Thanks for your picture and I bet we are the first twins born forty years apart."

562 Who was Millicent?

563 What happened to the boys' real mother?

564 Which Brady hung by his/her fingertips from the girls' bedroom window?

565 Why did Bobby tell Carol, "My whole class hates me!"?

566 Who was Skip Farnum?

567 What style was Greg referring to when he told Marcia, "The new Greg Brady style is supposed to be weird . . . really weird!"?

568 Who said, "Why does this always happen to me? People always forgetting who I am"?

569 Jan to Marcia: "Well, at least I had the courage to try your advice, and Dad's too . . . about the audience in their _____."

570 Who said, "But Alice, you always fix my knees and elbows and things"?

571 Who said, "Boys? Who likes boys?"

572 Why did Mike have to reschedule the family outing on his boss's boat?

573 Marcia: "On the way to the library I was passing Haskell's _____ Hut and Mr. Haskell was putting up a sign in the window. Help Wanted."

574 What did Mike's boss, Mr. Matthews, send Mike as a gift of appreciation for a job well done?

575 Why did Marcia tell Greg, "We can't let our parents read that paper!"?

576 Who was Bobby referring to when he told Oliver, "I wonder what in the world he wants to see my dad for"?

577 Alice: "You're going to love my cousin _____."

578 What did Carol sculpt that won third prize in an art competition before it got smashed to pieces?

579 What was Carol's dilemma her first Christmas with Mike?

580 What was Peter referring to when he asked Bobby, "Do you know what we just saw?"

581 What was Cindy referring to when she came home screaming, "I got it! I got it! Mary Ditmeyer thought she was but she didn't! I got it! I got it! I got it!"?

582 Which Brady tried out for but did not make the school Glee Club?

583 What was the significance of, "A strange woman will come into your life"?

584 What was Marcia referring to when she said, "We'll have to get someone this week or we'll have to tell Miss Robins that we bombed out"?

585 Where did Peter meet his double?

586 What was Peter referring to when he said, "So they can build a dumb old building on it"?

587 Who said, "I don't think I know anybody named Makr Maldrill"?

588 Who told Carol, "You see, I made the football team at school"?

589 Who was Alice referring to when she said, "Well, if you haven't seen her in years, don't be surprised if some of her go, go, go, is gone, gone, gone"?

590 To the best of your knowledge, how many toilets did the Bradys have?

591 What was Marcia referring to when she said, "Cindy, I'm going to win this fair and square, brother or no brother"?

592 What were the boys doing when they found a lost wallet?

593 Who was Peter talking about when he told his friends, "And we don't have to make him a regular member if he's willing to be our mascot"?

594 Why did Mike take the family to Cincinnati?

595 What part in the school play did Peter try out for, only to be cast as Benedict Arnold?

596 To whom did Bobby say, "You're going to drive me and Spunker to the frog-jumping contest on Saturday, aren't you?"

597 Why did Greg take a part-time job in Mike's office?

598 Why did Greg decide to buy hair tonic from Bobby?

599 Who said, "Here's what it says in the dictionary. To share: to divide into fair and equal portions"?

600 Who said, "What a beautiful little box. And inside the box . . . "?

601 Carol: "Okay, Greg and Marcia. You heard that. No nose blowing for _____."

602 Who said, "If that hound snitches one more thing, I'm going to ship him off to Siberia!"?

603 To whom did Marcia say, "You know who, about you know what, and about you know who. Now it'll be all over you know where and I'll die of humiliation!"?

604 Who complained, "I never have any privacy because I have too many brothers and sisters!"?

605 What was the big dilemma in the Brady household when all the kids came down with the measles at once?

606 What did Greg do for his history class project about the pilgrims?

607 Why did Alice say, "His name was Myron? I'm a murderess"?

608 What was Carol writing when Mike found her in his den at 1:45 in the morning?

609 Which Brady girl was a Sunflower Girl?

610 To whom did Peter say, "And when Westdale finds out that *my* sister's a double agent, they might not even let me in!"?

611 What idea was Kathy Kelly referring to when she told her husband, "That was Carol Brady on the phone. I was telling her about how lonesome Matt was and we came up with a terrific idea!"?

612 What was Carol referring to when she told Mike, "I merely found out that we're going to have an addition to the family"?

613 Why did Peter write a nice article about his science teacher in the school paper?

614 For what office did Greg and Marcia run against each other?

615 Why did Marcia think Alan Anthony *really* canceled his date with her to the school dance?

616 How did Marcia get Harvey Klinger to notice her?

617 To whom did Mike say, "Well, listen, Bub. Before you start spending all that money, you'd better realize that out of a thousand young hopefuls, only one makes it"?

618 What was the name of the Bradys' tour guide while in Hawaii?

619 Why did Bobby pretend to be Cindy's secret admirer?

620 Who was Mike referring to when he said, "He knows better than to bring a cap gun to school"?

621 Which Bradys weren't invited to Aunt Gertrude's wedding?

622 Greg to Marcia: "You outscored everybody in _____? Even the guys?"

623 Which three Brady kids had a part in the school play *Romeo and Juliet*?

624 Who was Bobby referring to when he told Cindy, "She hasn't got any feelings; she's full of sawdust or rags or something"?

625 Who said, "Then I carefully looked out the back window to make sure everything was clear"?

626 Which Brady kid joined the school Science Club and constructed a working volcano?

627 Who said, "I got fired"?

628 Greg to Carol: "I've been up in my room all afternoon working on this sure-fire hit _____"?

629 What excuse did Marcia give Charlie for breaking their date so she could go out with another guy?

630 Who complained, "Yuck! My crummy face! Greg was right—rotten freckles!"?

631 What did Zacchariah T. Brown, the old-timer the Bradys met on their way to the Grand Canyon, do to keep the Bradys from stealing his claim?

632 Who said, "That wasn't just a girl, that was an agent!"?

633 Who asked Sandra Martin, "Wait a minute. How old is your cousin Linda?"

634 Why did Peter say to Bobby, "Those pots?! That could have been my head!"?

635 Which Bradys said in unison, "It's *my* room and I'm not budging!"?

636 Marcia's dream of dreams was to be Mrs. _____?

637 Who said, "Greg, have you read this poem that Mrs. Tuttle sent for me to recite on the Family Frolic Night?"

638 What was Greg referring to when he told Mike, "This place is real funky!"?

639 Which Brady threw pebbles at Kerry Hathaway's bedroom window?

640 Who told Marcia, "I had no idea when she asked me who'd been using it, *why* she wanted to know"?

641 Who yelled, "Anybody who thinks bowling balls make a rotten wedding gift doesn't have a whole lotta taste!"?

642 What was Carol referring to when she said, "Mike, there's got to be some explanation for all these strange sounds"?

643 What was Bobby referring to when he said, "*Big deal*. I got picked too. For my grade"?

644 To whom did Mike say, "He [Greg] thinks you're a combination of George Washington, Neil Armstrong, and the guy who invented pizza"?

645 Mike to Greg: "I want you to promise me one thing. Before you buy a _____, you let me look at it first."

646 Which Brady dreamed about being a world series baseball champion, a world champion speedboat racer, and a world champion skier?

647 What was the first family trip the Brady family went on together?

648 Who said, "Those aren't girls! Those are your sisters!"?

649 Mike to Carol: "Two _____ and it's worse than it was before."

650 What was Bobby referring to when he said, "This is going to be the best booth in the whole school carnival!"?

651 Which Brady wasn't at all happy about Aunt Jenny coming to visit?

652 Who spied Millicent kissing Bobby?

653 What was so special about Saturday when Alice said, "I don't blame you for being nervous, Mr. Brady. This is a very important Saturday"?

654 Who saved Bobby from falling off the side of the house?

655 On what occasion did Cindy ask Carol, "If we're all going to be so happy, how come your eyes look like they're going to cry?"

656 Who said, "*Safety* monitor? SM should stand for *snitch* monitor"?

657 Where were the Bradys when they were approached by a TV director to do a commercial?

658 Who said, "I'm going to be a model. They get to wear all those long dresses with ostrich feathers and stuff"?

659 What was Marcia referring to when she told Jan, "She made a mistake and put my name instead of yours"?

660 Who whined, "Marcia, Marcia, Marcia!"?

661 Where did Cindy put Carol's earrings, which she borrowed without asking, when Carol suddenly knocked on the bathroom door?

662 Who was Alice referring to when she told Bobby, "You know, you're not very smart. You had a chance at a pretty nurse and you blew it"?

663 Why did the boys put itching powder in the sleeping bags?

664 Who was Dr. Howard referring to when he said, "Check them into the hospital before six, Friday afternoon"?

665 Who was Peter referring to when he said, "I don't get it. I wear out a pair of bike tires looking for a job all over town and one falls right into her lap"?

666 Mike: "Who would send me a _____?"

667 Who received a letter that began, "We have a terrible problem in my family"?

668 Who yelled, "Move it! Out of the sack! Hut two, hut two! Suit up and face out in the yard in fifteen minutes!"?

669 What was Myrna Carter doing when she told Mike and Carol, "Important?! Oh wow! Like motivation is everything!"?

670 Peter: "Nobody in my school believes I saw a _____."

671 Who said, "And I'm going to get the most applause 'cause I have the most family"?

672 What was Peter referring to when he said, "They had tryouts today and we [Peter, Jan, and Cindy] were picked"?

673 Harvey Klinger: "Gee, Marcia, you really know your _____."

674 Who said, "Back to the family room and another letter to my sister. She'll drop dead. Two letters from me in the same century?!"

675 Jan: "Myron wasn't exterminated! He's in the _____ upstairs in our room!"

676 Who was Marcia referring to when she said, "Wouldn't that be something? To get him to entertain at our prom?"

677 What was the name of the company that asked the Bradys to be in a commercial?

678 What was the name of Marcia's dentist before Dr. Vogel?

679 Who said "I'm about as graceful in ballet slippers as an elephant is in ice skates"?

680 What was Carol referring to when she told Mike, "Well, I was right there. But when she told everybody that we'd do it, well, they all stood up and applauded and said they'd get a theater, sell tickets, anything"?

681 Carol: "But the city owns that _____. Who would put a building on city property?"

682 Who was Mark Millard?

683 Who told Carol, "I'd be glad to quit math if you think it's too dangerous"?

684 Who was Carol referring to when she said, "I guess at her age a good man is hard to find"?

685 Who did Alan Melvin play?

686 What was Alice trying to teach Carol when she gave the following instructions: "With toes pointed outward, slightly squat, bend at the waist, pivot hips to the right, shoulder under the chin . . . "?

687 Who was with Bobby when he found a lost wallet?

688 What was Peter referring to when he said, "Okay, Bobby, we just voted you in"?

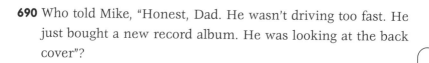

689 Where were the Bradys when Mike said, "Kids! I'll tell you what. Just remember that we meet back at the main restaurant at noon, sharp"?

690 Who told Mike, "Honest, Dad. He wasn't driving too fast. He just bought a new record album. He was looking at the back cover"?

691 What happened to the plans Mike gave Greg to deliver to the printer on his first day on the job?

692 Who did Bobby recruit to help him sell his hair tonic?

693 What item was Mike referring to when he said, "The truck driver's contest has an electric beeper. We have something a little more primitive"?

694 What was in the mysterious package sent to Jan?

695 Why did Mike tell Bobby, "Now, I'm going to go outside and knock on the door"?

696 Who said, "You know that certificate I didn't get? Well, I've got to get it over to Lloyd's Stereo Center before midnight tonight or it expires"?

697 To whom did Mike say, "From what we've been able to learn, there's a security leak in the Brady administration. *You* seem to come off as Mr. Know-it-all"?

698 What was Jan referring to when she told Marcia, "You were just scared because it was your first try"?

699 Who complained, "I have to live with five brothers and sisters all day, everyday"?

700 Why did Carol Call Dr. Porter?

701 Who said, "Listen! I'm the director and I say you're both going to be pilgrims!"?

702 Who told Alice, "It's only a plastic ink spot!"?

703 Which Brady boy joined the Sunflower Girls?

704 Who said, "Imagine hearing from Tank Gates after all these years"?

705 What was Kathy Kelly referring to when she told her husband, "It should be much easier this time. I mean, we've been through all of that red tape with Matt. We've filled out all those forms and everything"?

706 Carol to Mike: "It's my nephew _____. Can he come and stay with us for a while?"

707 What was Mike referring to when he said, "There's a simple answer that will make everyone happy. Split them up"?

708 To whom did Marcia say, "Hi and bye, small fry!"?

709 What did Peter break while playing ball in the house?

710 Which Brady boy defended Cindy from Buddy Hinton's teasing?

711 What was Peter's pen name when he wrote a column for his school paper?

712 Who said, "Greg took the plan for my campaign slogans! I left them here and they were gone this morning!"?

713 Who looked in the mirror and said, "I'm ugly, ugly, ugly!"?

714 Who asked, "Alice, have you ever been in love? I mean really, truly in love?"

715 Who said to Mike on his wedding day, "So you decided to show up after all!"?

716 Carol to Mike: "Do you realize that in the past month I've had to help _____ get her water fun badge, her foot traveler's badge, her Gypsy badge, and this morning, her Daniel Boone badge?"

717 Who asked, "Can't I even spit out the toothpaste?"

718 Peter: "Fighting's dumb _____. Let's try reasoning together."

719 Cindy: "I want Mommy to get her _____ back."

720 Who said, "Come on, Tiger. You're the only one around here who cares about me"?

721 Mike to Carol: "That's why he's flunking _____. Puppy love!"

722 Who was Bobby referring to when he said, "Boy, we never would have met them if it hadn't have been for my good luck charm"?

723 Who wrote, "When I think of your face and awful cute dimples, from head to toe, I get goose pimples"?

724 What parts did Peter and Jan play in the school production of *Romeo and Juliet*?

725 Which Brady did Carol and Alice initially think Jan was allergic to?

726 Who said, "Well, I just walked into the other room to toot my kazoo, 'cause I like to walk when I toot"?

727 Why did Carol get sued?

728 Who explained, "And when it erupts, smoke's gonna come out and real molten lava's gonna ooze all over the place"?

729 What was Mrs. Spencer referring to when she told Peter, "That was a very brave thing to do"?

730 Who told Marcia, "Something suddenly came up"?

731 Who was Alice referring to when she said, "We'll be planning her surprise birthday party for Saturday night"?

732 What happened to Bobby and Cindy after they chased an Indian boy in the Grand Canyon?

733 Tami Cutler to Greg: "Did anyone ever tell you your _____ would look great on an album cover?"

734 Why did Bobby say, "Who cares about the dumb old pots! What about me?!"

735 Why did Marcia say, "Why should I be penalized for being born a year too late?"

736 Who said, "Hey mister, you forgot this one. We might as well get rid of all the old books"?

737 Who said, "It's hard to believe that was once my room!"?

738 What happened when Peter tried to carry Kerry Hathaway's books for her at school?

739 Why did the Brady kids start giving Alice the cold shoulder?

740 Who said, "Well, as far as I'm concerned, Clara can elope without me Sunday!"?

741 Marcia to Jan: "I'd rather teach _____ a good lesson for snooping."

742 What was Carol referring to when she asked Bobby and Cindy, "*Both* of you got picked?"

743 Where and what was Greg doing when he met Don Drysdale?

744 To whom did Mike say, "You know what I see? I see a fellow who had a crummy time at a party"?

745 Bobby to himself: "I just gotta get a _____. I just gotta."

746 Why did Carol read the following books: *Rudiments of Baseball; Tips from Ruth to Mayes;* and *Baseball, the Art of Offense and Defense?*

747 Why didn't the Bradys catch any fish on their first camping trip together?

748 Who ran around the house screaming, "Mom's going to have a baby! Mom's going to have a baby!"?

749 Who said, "Fifty cents is mine. I lended it from Marcia"?

750 What was Carol referring to when she told Mike, "If Alice hurt herself, maybe I should come right back"?

751 Mike: "Now you kids have the _____ in here and *that's* the one you use."

752 What was Alice referring to when she said, "Believe me, when you hit that bulls eye . . . *SPLAT!*"?

753 Who was Jan referring to when she said, "I can't wait to find out what she looks like!"?

754 What was Cindy referring to when she ran around to the other kids singing, "I've got a secret! I've got a secret!"?

755 Why did Mike say, "I know it's an important Saturday. Who said I'm nervous? I'm mature and logical, and I know I'm doing the right thing"?

756 Why did Jan try out for the pompom girls?

757 Who said, "Greg? Greg? You saved my life"?

758 What was Bobby referring to when he said, "It means I have to fink on all my friends"?

759 What was Jan referring to when she told Alfred Bailey, "I'm glad you were able to get all of our names on it"?

760 Who followed the Bradys around the supermarket parking lot before finally approaching them?

761 Who told Alice, "I'm going to be an astronaut. Probably the first man on Mars. From now on, I'd better eat what they do. You know, all that powdered junk"?

762 Why did Carol want to wear the earrings she had loaned to Marcia?

763 Who was Alice referring to when she told Mike, "Sure she is. I bet she's a heck of a good button-sewer-onner"?

764 What was Carol referring to when she said, "Well, maybe we better hang them up and beat them"?

765 Who was the first Brady to work at Haskell's Ice Cream Hut?

766 Why did Carol say, "So long, bikini, I'm going to trade you in for some long underwear"?

767 What was Mike's boss, Mr. Matthews, referring to when he told Mike, "You know, I've got mine right smack dab in the middle of the living room. It might not be a bad place for yours"?

768 What letter was Alice referring to when she said, "He wouldn't write a letter like that in a million years"?

769 Who told Cousin Oliver, "Well, I'm working on a big project myself. That's how come I've got to see your uncle"?

770 Who was Mike referring to when he said to Carol, "Boy, she really has the kids hustling"?

771 What was Mike referring to when he told Greg, "Well, I'm surprised your school took it lying down, 'cause in my day *we* would have gone right out and stolen theirs"?

772 What happened to Carol's sculpture of Mike's head?

773 Who said, "Poor Victor. Poor Prince Victor. I shall never see him again"?

774 To whom did Mike say, "Hey, maybe you should play an instrument"?

775 What fan club was Marcia the president of?

776 Who did Mike set up with his boss's niece Pamela?

777 Why did Greg yell, "Be there, Dopey baby!"?

778 What was Greg referring to when he said, "After all the trouble we've gone to, to keep our park clean"?

779 Who was Carol referring to when she told Alice, "And to think he's called you after all these years"?

780 Who set up Great Grandma Hutchins with Great Grandpa Brady?

781 How many different bosses did Mike have throughout the series?

782 What was Greg's date referring to when she told Mike and Carol, "Oh, at first I was terrified. But when you're with someone so strong and capable . . . "?

783 What was Greg referring to when he said, "That's the third time you've looked through that. There's no identification in there"?

784 To whom did Greg say, "I'm going to keep throwing till you tell me your name"?

785 Which Bradys entered a frog-jumping contest?

786 What was Greg referring to when he said, "Dad got Mr. Phillips to give me another chance"?

787 Where did Bobby get the nails the men used to build the girls' clubhouse?

788 Why did the Bradys want to find the typewriter that dropped its Ys?

789 Who was Carol referring to when she said, "Our little gossip columnist was at it again today"?

790 What was Peter referring to when he told the other kids, "So I'm sorry. What I did was dumb and stupid. But I really didn't mean any harm"?

791 Marcia to Greg: "The important thing is that we're both good, safe drivers. Not who knocked off the _____."

792 Why did Mike ask Jan, "Yes, but does your friend Donna have any brothers or sisters?"

793 Why did Mike call Dr. Cameron?

794 Who yelled, "Well, I don't want anymore help! I'm getting helped right out of everything I want to do! I want to write my own screenplay, design my own sets, choose my costumes, and pick the actors. Don't you see, it's my project? It *has* to be my work"?

795 Who said, "That came in my box of jokes too!"?

796 To whom did Mike say, "You can have this whole den to yourself until you finish that article"?

797 What was Greg referring to when he said, "How do you like that? The first time my sister [Marcia] gets on TV and she sounds like a kook"?

798 Who was Tank Gates?

799 Who was Ken Kelly?

800 Who said, "I should have moved in with you guys *years* ago!"?

801 What was the name of the trading stamps the Bradys collected?

802 Who said, "When everybody leaves and no one says good-bye, that ain't love"?

803 Who was the last Brady to confess to breaking Carol's favorite vase?

804 What happened when Peter tried to reason with Buddy Hinton?

805 Why did Greg yell, "You *were* my campaign manager! Now get lost, Rusty!"?

806 Marcia: "Oh, my _____!"

807 Greg to Marcia: "When Dad sees that, he's gotta say I don't belong in the _____ business."

808 What happened to the ukulele Bobby bought in Hawaii?

809 What did Bobby give his friend to be Cindy's secret admirer?

810 What was Alice referring to when she said, "They're out to set a world record, remember?"

811 To whom did Mike ask, "Does it bother you with Tiger here near you?"

812 What was Peter referring to when he said, "If Bobby didn't take it, Cindy shouldn't say he did"?

813 What was Mr. Driscoll referring to when he said, "Well, the newspapers are going to hear about *this* act of bravery"?

814 What was Greg referring to when he told Carol, "He wants a hundred and fifty bucks in advance! That's a lot of bread"?

815 Who was Mr. Phillips?

816 Who told the Bradys, "Me and Bessie want to welcome you to Cactus Creek"?

817 What was Marcia doing when she told Mike, "It was the only place I could find that was private. I'm sorry if I made you angry"?

818 What was Greg referring to when he told the rest of the kids, "She said I should come alone"?

819 Who was Sandra Martin referring to when she told Greg, "I haven't seen her in six years. She had pigtails and braces then"?

820 What was Greg referring to when he told Marcia, "Look, I know how you feel and I can't blame you. But I honestly think Mom and Dad made the fair decision"?

821 Why did Cindy give away Marcia's diary?

822 Greg: "Oh Mom, if Marcia's willing to go out on a limb with her _____, what have you got to lose?"

823 Who complained, "These clothes are too straight for high school"?

824 Who said, "You've got to help me, Kay. I mean as long as you're not working. You could fill in for me"?

825 To whom did Sam say, "You've got a tongue sharp enough to slice salami!"?

826 Why did Carol think Greg broke his promise to never smoke again?

827 Who said, "By writing something special in my diary. Something that will drive Cindy bananas!"?

828 Why did the Brady kids decide to haunt their house after they told Mike they wanted to move into a bigger one?

829 What was Carol referring to when she sarcastically commented, "Too bad Bobby's suffering from a lack of confidence"?

830 What was Don Drysdale doing at the Brady house?

831 Who asked, "Well, how would you like to be the fourth guy asked to a party?"

832 Who was Carol referring to when she said, "He's in a magazine selling contest"?

833 Whose air mattress sprung a leak on the family camping trip?

834 Carol: "Oh _____, guess who's here? Linda!"

835 What did Alice think happened to Tiger in the episode in which he ran away?

836 Mike: "I know it's the _____. Take a look at the grand total this month!"

837 Marcia: "Congratulations _____, you've just given the word *popular* a new meaning."

838 Who was Jan referring to when she said, "Don't you understand? If I look like *this* now, I'll look like *that* then"?

839 Why was Millicent in quarantine?

840 On what occasion did Alice tell Mike, "It's the first time I saw you take twenty-one spoons of sugar"?

841 Who was Alice referring to when she said, "Sam, what if I were to find you an instant delivery boy?"

842 Who stated, "There is to be no disorderly conduct in the halls. Especially at my post"?

843 Who was Greg referring to when he said, "That guy's been following us all over the market"?

844 Whom did Mike and Carol dress up as for a costume party?

845 Of the two times Alice decided to pack up and leave the Bradys, why did she want to leave the first time?

846 What was Marcia referring to when she said, "I didn't write her name or that remark"?

847 To whom did Peter say, "You fired me because you're power hungry!"?

848 What kind of cookies did Alice make to help Jan win the "Most Popular Girl" election?

849 What was Bobby referring to when he said, "You wouldn't think it was so dumb if you knew the finer points of the game . . . like I do"?

850 What column in the Bradys' daily newspaper was written by Elizabeth Carter?

851 Why did Mike say, "I get the terrible feeling we've all been drafted"?

852 Why did Cindy refer to the boys as "Those monsters!"?

853 Who told Santa Claus, "Oh, I don't want any toys"?

854 Why did Peter ask, "Mom, can we borrow your camera tonight?"

855 To whom did Carol say, "Honey, just because you aren't great at singing doesn't mean you aren't musical"?

856 What did Beebe Gallini want Mike to design for her?

857 Who wrote Marcia a letter stating that if he was ever in town, he'd be glad to help her out in any way he could?

858 To whom did Peter say, "Thanks to you I've got two dates. I'm really in a spot"?

859 Which dwarf did all the Brady kids want to play when they put on their own production of *Snow White and the Seven Dwarfs*?

860 Marcia to the boys: "Jan and I each made a pair of _____ for Cindy. We want to find out which one is best."

861 Who said, "I sort of half promised Mark, my friend, that I wouldn't make any other plans while he was here"?

862 What was Great Grandpa Brady's profession?

863 What was the name of Mike's second boss?

864 Why did Jennifer Nichols cozy up to Greg?

865 What was Greg referring to when he told Peter, "I'm the one who threw it [football], so you could miss it [football], so he could find it"?

866 What did Greg want to do when he pleaded, "Dad, I'll drive *straight* there and I'll come *straight* back home"?

867 Who was Mike's boss, Mr. Phillips, referring to when he said, "Nice boy. Cleans a mean wastebasket"?

868 Why did the girls paint all over one another's shirts while wearing them in a particular episode?

869 What was Greg referring to when he told Mike, "Look, Dad! Look what they did! Curtains! They totaled the place!"?

870 Who answered, "Brushing my teeth. I forgot earlier and teeth can't tell time"?

871 To whom did Mike yell, "You didn't chain the door!"?

872 Who said, "Hey, Cindy! Guess what! I won a prize in the jingle contest!"?

873 What was Greg referring to when he told Peter, "All right, Mr. Big Ears! Haven't you learned your lesson yet? Marcia found *this* under her desk, and it was going!"?

874 Who said, "What kills me is that Molly beat me with a speech that *I* helped her write"?

875 What problem was Cindy referring to when she told Jan, "We're supposed to be nice to you till you get over your problem. Then we can forget about you again"?

876 What happened when Dr. Porter met Dr. Cameron?

877 Who said, "Mom! Dad! That groovy history teacher gave me an *A* for the movie!"?

878 What was Carol referring to when she said, "It's my story. He sent it back"?

879 Who was Jerry Rogers?

880 Who were Matt, Dwayne, and Steve?

881 Carol: "Oh Mike, I think _____ is going to be very happy here."

882 What was Greg referring to when he said, "You know, I'll bet we looked through this catalog five times"?

883 Who was Alice referring to when she said, "One of your little chickadees is about to fly the coop"?

884 Who was Carol referring to when she told Mike, "Correction. *six* suspects. And number six is looking forward to an overnight camping trip this Saturday"?

885 Who said, "Gee, Buddy, I'm sorry. I didn't mean to hurt you"?

886 To whom did Greg say, "You didn't mention a single name. Kids like to see their names in the paper, to read about themselves"?

887 What did Marcia do when it came time to read her election speech for student body president?

888 Who said, "Dust makes my eyes red . . . which is very unbecoming to a woman going steady"?

889 Why did Bobby give Greg the little tiki idol he found in Hawaii?

890 Who said, "Gee, Harvey! Gosh!"?

891 Who was Cindy referring to when she said, "She's hugging the postman! I'm positive, she's hugging the postman!"?

892 At what occasion did Carol yell, "Girls! Stop that screaming right now!"?

893 What was Cindy wearing when Bobby told Alice, "When I get to three, I'm going to scalp her!"?

894 Who read, "It means that other students believe that I have more charm and personality than anyone in the class"?

895 Who said, "This is a queen. No wings you'll notice. She pulled them off herself. Though why? Why? One of the eternal mysteries of the insect world"?

896 Carol: "Bobby, did you know that almost everything _____ did was against the law?"

897 What was Carol referring to when she asked Alice, "You don't mean to tell me they're still on that thing?"

898 To whom did Carol say, "You don't have to tell me, your team lost the debate"?

899 Who was Carol referring to when she said, "If only she didn't think she was junior high's answer to Sarah Bernhardt"?

900 Why did the Bradys think they had to get rid of Tiger?

901 To whom was Marcia referring to when she told Greg, "Let's give him a fair trial. *Then* we'll hang him"?

902 Greg to Mike and Carol: "Hey, who banged up the _____?"

903 What was Mike referring to when he told Jan, "We've got the cylinders mixed up. Where is yours?"

904 What award did a newspaper reporter and photographer present Peter with?

905 To whom did Peter say, "Mr. Dimsdale gave me some good advice. He said that family groups sell millions of records"?

906 To whom did the druggist say, "I suppose these freckles she has are a real big problem"?

907 Who wrote, "Even when he punishes me, it's because I deserve it"?

908 Who said, "Look, I can go down and make the deal for all of us. Okay?"

909 Carol to Mike: "Greg's trying to get a date for his date's _____."

910 To whom did Greg say, "If Marcia's willing to go out on a limb with her voice, what have you got to lose?"

911 Who was told, "Well, maybe next year. You know, you're really going to be kind of cute when you grow up"?

912 Who screamed, "It's dark again!"?

913 Who said, "No, it's not what I want, it's what's best. And the sooner I leave, the better"?

914 Where was Jan when she destroyed the portrait of the children Mike had hidden away until his and Carol's anniversary?

915 What was Greg referring to when he said, "It's no use Alice. All the evidence points toward me. Even if I'm not guilty"?

916 What was the significance of, "Something fantastic might be happening for Cindy. I don't dare tell her because I don't want her to get her hopes up too high. But I told all the other kids and Alice and swore them to secrecy. More later"?

917 Who was Marcia referring to when she told Carol, "He came into this room while I was dressing! He didn't even knock or anything! He just barged in!"?

918 Who said, "I'm building a real Indian teepee"?

919 Which Brady played in the Pony League?

920 Bobby to Cindy: "Wait till I tell Mom and Dad I sold _____ to a lot of their friends."

921 Why did Mike read the following books: *How to Cook in Thirty Easy Lessons, Cooking Can Be Fun,* and *You Too Can Be a Chef*?

922 Carol to Mike: "You'll have to forgive us, Honey. It's our first night of _____ and we're just a little nervous."

923 Who said, "I halfway expected to see Greg chained to one of your desks"?

924 Who was Mike referring to when he said, "Peter found him?! Good! We're on our way!"?

925 Why were all the kids put in charge of *all* the household chores in one particular episode?

926 What was Mike referring to when he told Carol and Alice, "Excuse me while I show this bill to a certain group of children"?

927 What was Bobby referring to when he told Millicent, "It'll be our secret. Nobody else will ever know"?

928 Who was Mike referring to when he told the boys, "That makes it unanimous. *I* think she's pretty special too"?

929 Who said, "My essay won ninety-eight out of a possible one hundred points!"?

930 Who said, "Six inches in one year? Wow, if I could do that . . . "?

931 Which Brady kid put too much laundry detergent in the washing machine?

932 The engraving for Mike and Carol's anniversary platter cost how much per letter?

933 Who was Jan referring to when she said, "Why does he keep looking at us through his hands?"

934 What was Mike referring to when he told Greg, "The correct equipment can make all the difference in the work you do"?

935 Why did Carol say, "Jan, I really think you're making too much of this. After all, you *are* the one invited to the party"?

936 To whom did Carol loan her favorite earrings, which wound up in the washing machine?

937 Who said, "Well, you see . . . what it really is . . . you see, I have this aunt of mine"?

938 Who said, "Well, I finished my classwork early and I was doodling and my name happened to be on the paper"?

939 Jan: "My _____, it's gone! I wore it to bed a couple hours ago, then something woke me up and I found out it was gone!"

940 On whom did Cindy tattle for coloring his skateboard with Carol's new lipstick?

941 Who said, "Oh, I've never been on a honeymoon!"?

942 Why did Bobby tell Alice, "I'm Little Owl, not her!"?

943 What was Mike referring to when he said, "Two weeks from Saturday would be better for us, Mr. Phillips, if that's okay with you"?

944 What was Marcia referring to when she said, "I've got an idea. I'll put the poster on the back of the car and I'll drive Jan around the neighborhood"?

945 What was Bobby referring to when he said, "Are you kidding? I could beat both those bums with one hand tied behind my back"?

946 Who was "Harried and Hopeless"?

947 Who said, "I need some plans, Mr. Brady. You see, the store next to mine is vacant, and Mr. Gronsky, he's my landlord, he told me that if I want to enlarge, he's going to give me first shot at it"?

948 Who said, "Listen, I thought it was the *artist* who was supposed to starve, not the model!"?

949 What was Bobby referring to when he told Peter, "Don't just lie there! Take pictures!"?

950 Why did Cindy ask the boys, "How do they hang me up?"

951 Who said, "Guess who we've got helping us at football practice today? Deacon Jones!"?

952 What was the Brady family doing when Bobby told Greg, "I didn't spit now 'cause I didn't spit then!"?

953 Who was Marcia referring to when she said, "If I said I'll get him, I'll get him!"?

954 Who said, "I have to pick up Michelle at seven o'clock, so get here a little before. And wear the same thing as me. A white tee shirt and blue jeans"?

955 Who said, "In fact, I have no talent for anything at all"?

956 What was Peter referring to when he said, "We'll do anything to save it"?

957 To whom did Greg say, "Next time, take a picture when they don't know it. Then they don't look stiff, they look natural"?

958 To whom did Connie Hutchins say, "You know, there's something I always wondered about judges. Is it true that on hot days, judges don't wear any pants under their robes?"

959 Which four Bradys wore braces?

960 Marcia: "I just wish there was some way we could settle this. I'd prove I'm as good a _____ as you are."

961 How did Bobby develop his fear of heights?

962 What was Jan referring to when she told Marcia, "I couldn't decide between a bear and a giraffe"?

963 Why did Peter say, "I'm getting fed up with everyone calling me a traitor!"?

964 What was Mike referring to when he told Carol, "I can't believe that Greg would deliberately disobey us"?

965 Who said, "I've got to find your husband, Mrs. Petersen! My whole future is in the back seat of his car!"?

966 What was Bobby referring to when he said, "It came! It came! This package! What's in this package is going to make me a million bucks!"?

967 What was Jan referring to when she said, "That's why I screamed. Only it wasn't a screamy scream, it was a happy scream"?

968 Why did Greg call the police the night Mike and Carol left he and Marcia to baby-sit?

969 Who said, "Co-hostesses? You mean . . . me and you?"

970 To whom did Greg say, "As far as you're concerned, we don't even exist! Consider us invisible!"?

971 Who was Dr. Porter?

972 Who was Greg referring to when he said, "He's my science project"?

973 Why did Carol say, "Mike, I've been rejected. Flatly rejected"?

974 Who said, "Oh no! Not me! I'm not going to be any Sunflower Girl!"?

975 Why did Jerry Rogers start dating Marcia?

976 To whom did Mrs. Payne say, "I see you now have several children . . . of various colors, one might say"?

977 Who was convinced he was a jinx?

978 What was Carol referring to when she told Mike and Alice, "On no! This family better make up its mind and quick!"?

979 To whom did Bobby say, "As soon as I get somewhere, I'll send for you"?

980 Why couldn't Peter go on his first camping trip with just the guys?

981 Who was Mike referring to when he said, "I'm just going to reason with him. Reasoning. Calm, cool reasoning"?

982 To whom did Marcia say, "The easiest way to remember something is to make up little rhymes about them. Like 'a vertebrate has a back that's straight'"?

983 What was Marcia referring to when she ran home from school saying, "Mother! They nominated me! I couldn't believe it, but they did!"?

984 Why did Marcia scream, "I hate you, Alan Anthony! I hate everybody!"?

985 Who said, "When I imagined the whole audience in their underwear, I could hardly keep from laughing!"?

986 What was Marcia referring to when she said, "I don't know why you're knocking yourself out, Bobby. Greg can beat you with one hand tied behind his back"?

987 To whom did Mike say, "Listen, right now he may seem like a very colorful Western character to you"?

988 What was Carol referring to when she said, "You've got to promise me one thing, kids. That you'll both stop when you get tired"?

989 To whom did Marcia say, "You were just afraid because it was your first face-to-face debate"?

990 What was Marcia referring to when she said, "Mom, do you think they'd let me do it? I'll learn the lines real fast, word for word. And I won't cause any trouble, I promise"?

991 Why did the Bradys hold a mock trial in the living room?

992 What was Greg referring to when he told Mike, "Marcia shouldn't have any problem. I mean, she's a cool chick"?

993 What was Peter referring to when he yelled, "Mom! Dad! Mom! Dad! It happened! It happened!"?

994 Who said, "Me? A hero? Come on!"?

995 Who asked Marcia and Jan to sing the word *no?*

996 Who told Marcia the best way to break a date is to say, "Something suddenly came up"?

997 Who said, "There goes your last excuse. It isn't your freckles! It's just dumb old you!"?

998 To whom did Mike say, "Goodnight. And no more going out the window!"?

999 Who was Buddy Berkman referring to when he told his partner, "I hope he fits the suit"?

1000 To whom did Greg say, "Don't say too much. Be the strong, silent type. That way you can't make too many mistakes"?

1001 What was Greg referring to when he told Marcia, "No, I *want* you to have it. It has nothing to do with you being a blubbering idiot"?

1002 Who said, "My confidential, secret feelings in the hands of a complete stranger"?

1003 Who said, "With the songs the way they are nowadays, you can't hear the words well enough to understand that what you would have heard well enough to hear it anyway"?

1004 What grade was Greg in when he moved his room into Mike's den for a short period of time?

1005 What picture was Mike referring to when he told Jan, "Get the bike back fast because we have to get that picture taken before they get back from the dentist"?

1006 What was Carol referring to when she said, "Hey, you know, Peter? She'd make a real cute assistant for you"?

1007 Mike to Marcia: "You know, _____, some authorities say, wore braces."

1008 Jan: "What's happened is what I remembered. I completely forgot about _____."

1009 Who played Penelope Fletcher?

1010 Jan to Marcia: "No job is worth all this! I resign! Now maybe Mr. _____ will give you your job back!"

1011 What was Carol referring to when she asked, "How did you ever sneak out and get it done?"

1012 Jan to Greg: "I took him out of his _____ in your room last night, just to play a joke."

1013 Why did Cindy's rabbits turn orange?

1014 Who said, "It was a kind of kicky blast. The guys really got it together and really wailed and bent the gig out of shape"?

1015 Who played Carol's Aunt Jenny?

1016 Who said, "It's a muridae musmuscalous"?

1017 On which island did the Bradys stay in Hawaii?

1018 How many days did Peter work at his first job before getting fired?

1019 Where did the Bradys go for their annual family campouts?

1020 What was Jan referring to when she said, "We've been saving them ever since we were little kids"?

1021 What was the Brady's street address?

1022 Who said, "Oliver, do you know something about me that I don't know?"

1023 Why did Marcia break her date with Charley?

1024 Why did Greg invite Kathy Lawrence over to the house?

1025 Who said, "We'll have to get someone this week or we'll have to tell Miss Robbins that we bombed out"?

1026 Which Brady locked him/herself in the bedroom, not letting anyone in?

1027 How many chin-ups can Bobby do?

1028 Who said, "You know, baseball's been real good to me"?

1029 What kind of outfit was Skip Farnum wearing when he discovered the Bradys in the supermarket parking lot?

1030 What was the significance of, "Be a smart cookie. Vote for Jan Brady"?

1031 What was the name of the toy store where Peter saved a little girl's life?

1032 What did the Bradys have for dinner the day Peter tried out Humphrey Bogart's personality?

1033 Who said, "Guess what! Our school is putting on an old-time vaudeville show and I signed up for it!"?

1034 Where was Greg when he told Bobby, "I know you want to help, but there's only room for one up here"?

1035 What were Bobby and Oliver doing when the FBI agent came to see Mike on official business?

1036 What was Mr. Phillips's first name?

1037 Where was Alice when she told the kids, "I just got back to town. That other job I had didn't work out"?

1038 Greg to Pete Sterne: "Just call us 'The _____.' "

1039 Who did Bobby bribe to be Cindy's secret admirer?

1040 Whose favorite book was entitled *The Wonderful World of Insects*?

1041 Jan to Carol: "Do you expect *me* to sleep in a _____?"

1042 Who said, "Forgettin's easy. It's rememberin' that's hard"?

1043 What was Marcia referring to when she asked, "When is your great inner-sanctum going to be ready?"

1044 Who said, "What's wrong?! Everything's wrong! My whole class hates me!"?

1045 Who was Raquel?

1046 Against whom did Marcia compete for the title of hostess of Senior Banquet Night?

1047 Who was the last Brady to get the measles?

1048 Who said, "How do you like that? The first time my sister gets on TV and she sounds like a kook!"?

1049 What was the name of Peter's column in the school newspaper?

1050 Why did Mike, Carol, and Alice each invite a boy over to the house to see Marcia?

1051 What was Peter's line in the school play *Romeo and Juliet*?

1052 What was the title of Jan's essay on Americanism that won second place?

1053 Who complained, "I'll tell you what the problem is. You have to wait in line for everything around here! Someone's always borrowing your things!"?

1054 Which two Bradys awoke in the middle of the night to find a "ghost" outside their bedroom window?

1055 How much money was in the wallet Bobby found while playing football with his brothers?

1056 Who said, "God bless Mr. and Mrs. Kelly . . . I mean, Mom and Dad"?

1057 Who said, "He always has dinner at our house whenever he's in town"?

1058 Why did Marcia sneak out of her bedroom window in the middle of the night?

1059 What was Mike referring to when he told Carol, "Well, Honey, if the kids are going to do their part, I think the least the parents can do is theirs"?

1060 Who asked, "What's so funny about the word *bowling* lately?"

1061 What was the name of the Bradys' real estate agent, whom they hired to sell their house?

1062 Who said, "I'm going to buy it Dad . . . look, a hundred and nine dollars"?

1063 How did Alice find out that Greg had a crush on a girl named Linda?

1064 Who said, "A few years ago, I thought it was the end of the world"?

1065 Which Brady kids screamed, "Fire drill!" during Peter's party?

1066 What happened to Carol's favorite earrings after Cindy hid them under a towel in the bathroom?

1067 Who was Alice referring to when she said, "Well, I wouldn't go if I didn't know you had a first-rate pinch hitter for me"?

1068 Who said, "Boy, is Greg ever a good driver. We just missed getting into an accident!"?

1069 What part did all the girls want to play in Greg's movie about the pilgrims?

1070 What was Mike referring to when he told Carol, "Well, it's no big thing. But it's not exactly small, tiny, minor either"?

1071 Who said, "This is Clark Tyson. We're studying for a geography test together"?

1072 Which Brady came home with a trophy for being the best jacks player at the playground?

1073 What was Carol referring to when she told Mike, "It *does* look like hers. It's the same make, same color, everything"?

1074 To whom did Marcia say, "On the way to the library I was passing Haskell's Ice Cream Hut and Mr. Haskell was putting up a sign in the window: Help Wanted"?

1075 What was Carol's first married name?

1076 Who was Carol referring to when she told Alice, "All her symptoms have disappeared"?

1077 Who explained, "*That's* the moat"?

1078 What was the significance of a piece of paper that read "Makr Maldrill"?

1079 Carol: "Isn't it marvelous, Alice? My cousin _____ is finally getting married!"

1080 What was Marcia referring to when she said, "I wonder why he asked Dad and not me"?

1081 Which three Bradys were in the school Glee Club?

1082 What was Carol referring to when she told Mike and Greg, "Yeah, it's so great that both of you are too chicken to tell me what it is!"?

1083 Who was Jan referring to when she told Alice, "Old? Somehow I never think of her as old"?

1084 Who gave Greg the nickname "Greggy"?

1085 Did Millicent have the mumps?

1086 Why did Santa Claus tell Cindy that she was a sweet, unselfish little girl?

1087 Who was Marcia referring to when she said, "He has dark, gorgeous hair, dreamy eyes, groovy bell bottom pants, neat shoes . . . and he plays the best rock and roll music in his office!"?

1088 What was the name of the local park the Bradys fought to save?

1089 Who shouted, "Peter! Look out!"?

1090 Which Brady boy belonged to a treehouse club?

1091 What was the name of the televised talent show the Brady kids were auditioning for when Greg was discovered by an agent?

1092 Who told Carol and Alice, "There are different tests for different grades. And I got picked to take the test for my grade to see who gets picked to *be* on television"?

1093 What did Carol call Mr. Phillips's boat?

1094 What was Greg referring to when he told Marcia, "Are you kidding? Jerry's the opposition"?

1095 Marcia: "My dream of dreams is to be Mrs. _____."

1096 In which season did Cindy lose her pigtails?

1097 Marcia: "Dad, unless there's a very good reason why I can't, I want to join Greg's _____."

1098 Marcia: "I doodled _____, I didn't doodle Mrs. Denton!"

1099 Why did Alice hug the postman?

1100 Who was Fluffy?

1101 Mike to Bobby: "If you had to get the _____, you got them the best way you could get them."

1102 For what office did both Greg and Marcia run at the same time?

1103 Bobby to Greg: "Can't I even spit out the _____?"

1104 What was Sam's last name?

1105 What was Greg referring to when he said, "Looks like we have a three-way tie. In the event of a three-way tie, the chairman decides it. That's me"?

1106 Cindy: "Dr. Porter gives all-day _____!"

1107 Mike: "That's why he's flunking math . . . _____!"

1108 Jan to Greg and Bobby: "What's so funny about my _____?"

1109 Carol: "You asked _____ to give me my voice back?"

1110 Who said, "Now how do I convince the doctor that I'm sick?"

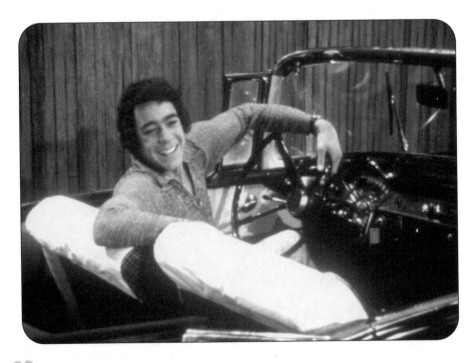

1111 Who was the astronaut who appeared in the episode in which Peter and Bobby were convinced they saw a UFO?

1112 Who said, "We may as well face it, there's no hope for me. The picture proves it"?

1113 Who said, "I'll never do it again! I'll never play another joke as long as I live!"?

1114 What was Bobby referring to when he said, "Hey Pete! Look what I found! It's real old!"?

1115 What was Marcia referring to when she told Mike and Carol, "Every time *they* wanted something, *we* wanted something else"?

1116 Who said, "Kitty? Kitty? Kitty? Where are you?"

1117 Who was Greg referring to when he said, "She didn't even say good-bye"?

1118 What was Greg referring to when he said, "Make up your mind, Ronnie. Is it a deal?"

1119 What was Jan referring to when she told Marcia, "Let's catch her in the act!"?

1120 Who was Jimmy Pakaya?

1121 What was Peter referring to when he said, "Gee, something spectacular like this could be the highlight of my act"?

1122 What was Marcia referring to when she said, "I was so shook up by Doug that I completely forgot"?

1123 To whom did Greg say, "You'll be perfectly safe. These are real strong belts"?

1124 Why did Marcia's teacher and all of her girlfriends swarm around her one morning at school?

1125 Who said, "Mr. Dimsdale gave me some good advice. He said that family groups sell millions of records"?

1126 Who was Bobo?

1127 During which season did Mike go perm?

1128 What position did Greg play in the Pony League?

1129 What was the title of the article written about Peter in the local newspaper?

1130 Why did Alice lie to Carol and say she had a toothache?

1131 Who said, "A star can't go on television all fat and broken out"?

1132 Who was Carol referring to when she said to Alice, "Uh oh, someone sure hit a clinker"?

1133 What apparatus was Bobby on when he said, "I'll bet I'm getting longer by the minute"?

1134 What color and make were the six cars Mike owned?

1135 What were Romeo and Julius?

1136 On whose coat did Jan stick a plastic ink spot as a practical joke?

1137 Who found Bobby's lost tiki statue in the hotel hallway?

1138 Peter: "_____ says I'm not mechanically inclined."

1139 What was Mike referring to when he said, "Bob, it isn't the grade. What we're interested in is how you happened to write it"?

1140 Why did Carol say, "Mike, how about your den?"

1141 Carol to Jan: "You don't have to tell me, your team lost the _____."

1142 What was Mike referring to when he told the kids, "Split them up"?

1143 What were the Brady kids doing when Cindy said, "Well, Kitty's gone and Bobby took her 'cause no one else was there. And those are my exact words"?

1144 What was Carol referring to when she said, "Alice, what am I going to tell the children. They'll be heartbroken"?

1145 What constellation was Jan looking at the night she lost her mysterious little locket?

1146 Why did Marcia and Jan spy on Cindy from behind the bathroom door?

1147 Who told Kerry Hathaway, "Pleased to meet me"?

1148 Who was Carol referring to when she asked Marcia, "Wasn't he at the hotel?"

1149 What was Jan playing with in the backyard that went crashing through the family room window?

1150 Where were the Bradys when Carol said, "Just ignore him and let's get going"?

1151 Who said, "Wouldn't it be nice if Bobby got into the back seat to eat his pizza?"

1152 What was Jan referring to when she said, "I'm sorry about the bike mix-up, Dad. I guess I was in such a hurry to get home that I didn't look close enough"?

1153 Who said, "That call was from some kid in your class named Herman. He's got some stupid idea that *I'm* going to help him with his algebra"?

1154 Beebe Gallini to Mike: "There is only one thing that I ask. That it should be _____."

1155 Which Brady kids held part-time jobs at one time or another?

1156 Why did Alice ask Sam, "Let the postman take me? What's that supposed to mean?"

1157 What was Carol referring to when she told Mike, "They sure are giving it everything they've got"?

1158 Where did Peter find Tiger?

1159 To whom did Alice say, "I think Cindy makes a heap pretty squaw"?

1160 To whom did Cindy say, "I got your flowers and candy and big diamond ring"?

1161 What was Greg referring to when he told Marcia, "Why not give him something to really listen to?"

1162 What happened to Buddy Hinton when Peter hit him?

1163 Who said, "Oh Musketomestici! I love you!"?

1164 What did the girls do to scare the boys on their first camping trip?

1165 Why did Marcia say, "But there's another thing we did when Alice sprained her ankle. We sprained Alice's love life too"?

1166 To whom did all the Bradys write letters inquiring about "Harried and Hopeless"?

1167 Why did Mike say to Carol, "Maybe we should write a nasty letter to the fairy tale control board"?

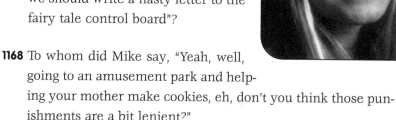

1168 To whom did Mike say, "Yeah, well, going to an amusement park and help- ing your mother make cookies, eh, don't you think those pun- ishments are a bit lenient?"

1169 What was the name of the little girl who asked Bobby to res- cue her cat from an old, abandoned house?

1170 What was Greg referring to when he said, "Dad, I was stuck. There was no place else I could take her"?

1171 Why couldn't Greg join the Sunflower Girls?

1172 Who told Peter, "Vanity is what makes women with size twelve feet wear size eight shoes"?

1173 Why did Alan Anthony break his date with Marcia to go to the school dance?

1174 What part was Marcia referring to when she said, "I just don't think I should play the part"?

1175 Who was Nora Cooms?

1176 To whom did Peter say, "You made a date with Pamela, right? Well, you're going to keep that date and I'm going to keep my date with Michelle"?

1177 Who was Mike referring to when he told Carol, "His laryngitis seems to have cured his ankle"?

1178 Who was Randi Petersen?

1179 To what event was Marcia referring when she said, "I hope Jan changes her mind and decides to come with us"?

1180 Why did Cindy say, "We want to borrow some money from your rich, friendly bank"?

1181 To whom did Marcia say, "I almost didn't have this party because of what you wrote"?

1182 Who said, "Let me out, I'm burning up. I must rise and walk the night"?

1183 What was Alice referring to when she said, "Are you ready for plaid cowhide?"

1184 What was Steve Kelly's ethnic background?

1185 To whom did Cindy say, "I'm sorry, too. I wrote the letter"?

1186 What was Marcia referring to when she told Jan, "I've got a real big secret, but if I don't tell someone soon, I'm simply going to bust!"?

1187 Mike: "Greg, have you read this _____ that Mrs. Tuttle sent for me to recite?"

1188 Why did Mrs. Huntsicker say, "I must say, you people celebrate Halloween at a strange time of year"?

1189 Who said, "What hole? A little rip. Just sew it up. Only a dime for needle and thread"?

1190 What was the name of Greg's math teacher on whom he had a crush?

1191 Who said, "The cigarettes weren't Greg's. They're mine"?

1192 What was Mike referring to when he said, "We ought to do something to show Mr. Matthews our appreciation for the gift"?

1193 Who asked, "Have you ever read the army manual on mess hall organization?"

1194 Who was Spunker?

1195 Greg: "Mom, Dad, that groovy history teacher gave me an *A* for the _____."

1196 Who was Harry Duggan?

1197 Why did Cindy say, "I guess she wants sour skin"?

1198 Bobby to Mike and Carol: "You called up all your friends and told them to buy _____ from me!"

1199 What was Marcia referring to when she asked, "Suppose we end up in another tie?"

1200 Who said, "You fired me 'cause you're power hungry!"?

1201 Who told Carol, "That's what I was trying to tell you. We're running against each other"?

1202 Which two Bradys spied Greg smoking in the park with his friends?

1203 What were Mike and Carol referring to when they said, "Those poor boys; it'll break their hearts"?

1204 What was Mike referring to when he told Carol, "Oh *yes!* I thought that was the national debt!"?

1205 Who said, "It's fatal, and I've got it"?

1206 Who told Alice, "How could all these years have gone by and not touched you at all?"

1207 What was Oliver referring to when he said, "Gee, I'm sorry, Aunt Carol. It got tangled around my foot"?

1208 What did Carol buy her cousin Gertrude for her wedding gift?

1209 What was the name of the Hispanic couple Mike and Carol took out to dinner?

1210 What was Carol referring to when she said to Mike as they went out for the evening, "I'm just afraid she and Greg are going to have a big blow-up"?

1211 To whom did Peter say, "What do you mean, girls? There's guys in the Glee Club, too"?

1212 What were the Bradys doing while Bobby sat out and watched from the top of the stairs because he thought he might have the mumps?

1213 What did Carol wake up humming on Christmas morning?

1214 Who was Jan referring to when she told Marcia, "Hey, according to this article, he'd be perfect for you"?

1215 Mike to kids: "If that _____ is worth having, it's worth fighting for."

1216 Who said, "If it weren't for you, I wouldn't be polishing these shoes, I'd be polishing my harp at the pearly gates"?

1217 Who said, "A parakeet?! Gee, thanks Dad!"?

1218 How did Zacchariah T. Brown lure the Bradys into the old jail cell before locking them in?

1219 Who told the other kids, "She said I should come alone"?

1220 To whom did Carol say, "Lets face it, chum, you didn't pass because you didn't study"?

1221 What was Carol referring to when she said, "Well, that's impossible, Dr. Howard"?

1222 What kind of poster did Jan buy at the amusement park for Nancy, the girl she baby-sat?

1223 What was Carol referring to when she said, "Aw, be patient with her, kids. I'm sure after a few more lessons she'll get much better at it"?

1224 Who asked Marcia, "Don't I get some kind of reward for driving you home?"

1225 What was Greg referring to when he said, "Hey, wait a minute. There's seven dwarfs and only six of us. So there's still two slips of paper left"?

1226 Which Brady girl said, "I'm delighted to meet you, boys"?

1227 Who said, "I strung a piece of fishing line over the yard, between those two trees. Then I hid a clear plastic curtain behind one of the trees"?

1228 Who said, "I know! I saw an ad in the newspaper! We can make a fortune raising worms!"?

1229 Why did Jan sneak into the boys' room in the middle of the night?

1230 On which beach did the Bradys stay while in Hawaii?

1231 Peter: "I'll try harder, Mr. _____."

1232 What grade did Bobby get on his paper about Jesse James?

1233 Marcia: "Now that's a typical male chauvinist reaction. You're prejudiced against women _____."

1234 What was Carol referring to when she told Mike, "The important thing is, they are picking it out together"?

1235 Why did Carol tell Mike, "That's not fair. They're treating Bobby as if he were a criminal"?

1236 Who explained, "But two days ago, the woman who runs it up and eloped"?

1237 What was the name of the man who ran the theatre where the Bradys had originally planned to put on the play *Snow White and the Seven Dwarfs*?

1238 What did Charley deliver to the Bradys the day Marcia broke her date with him?

1239 Carol: "But Oliver, I thought you were all excited about going to the _____."

1240 Who asked, "Mr. Dimsdale? I wonder if that's *Johnny* Dimsdale's dad?"

1241 What was Sam referring to when he told Oliver, "Well, I'm working on a big project myself. That's how come I've got to see your uncle"?

1242 How many seasons did *The Brady Bunch* run?

1243 Greg to Peter: "What if I joined the _____? That would show her!"

1244 Cindy to Mike: "Okay, if you don't want to know that Bobby used Mommy's new lipstick to color his _____."

1245 Why did Alice tell Mike, "It's the first time I saw you take twenty-one spoons of sugar"?

1246 Marcia: "Dad, you don't call a _____ 'Sweetheart'."

1247 What two games did the girls play at Marcia's slumber party?

1248 What was Cindy referring to when she said, "Alice said to copy the letters, she didn't say how"?

1249 Mike to Carol: "Well, he couldn't lose those _____ again . . . he couldn't do that!"

1250 Alice to Carol: "My Uncle _____ called me last night and I wanted to tell you right then and there but I just couldn't."

1251 Marcia to Carol: "Like _____ says, parents just don't understand our generation!"

1252 From what pet store did Cindy buy her rabbits?

1253 What was the name of Greg's first high school band?

1254 Who said, "Balderdash! I got some bad vibrations in there! Now that child doesn't dig me and I'd like to know why!"?

1255 Who casually said, "Guess who Greg's got helping him in science? . . . *Myron!*"?

1256 Who said, "No! Do not touch! Taboo, taboo idol!"?

1257 To whom was the librarian referring to when she said, "As a matter of fact, we have several good books on his life"?

1258 What was Marcia referring to when she said, "Would you like to back that with a bet, Mr. Male Chauvinist?"

1259 What was Alice referring to when she pulled out a kitchen drawer and said, "Who gets custody of these?"

1260 Who explained, "She just asked me a question and I answered it"?

1261 What was Greg referring to when he said, "Three times . . . in Brady, Way, and in City"?

1262 Who exclaimed, "Wow! I ought to be a good private eye! I've got four of them!"?

1263 Who said, "Hello, lovely one"?

1264 Who jumped around the family room on all fours saying, "Ribit, ribit, ribit, ribit!"?

1265 Who wrote a letter to one of the Brady children, stating that if ever in town, he would be glad to do him/her any favor he could?

1266 Who was Alice referring to when she asked, "And he won't let anybody else in the room?"

1267 What was Greg doing when he met Don Drysdale?

1268 Against whom did Jan run for "Most Popular Girl"?

1269 What was the name of the little girl whose life Peter saved at the local toy store?

1270 Who pleaded, "Bring him back, Peter, please bring him back!"?

1271 What was Sam referring to when he said, "When the proper time does come, Alice, you'll be the first to know"?

1272 What two roles did Jim Backus play on *The Brady Bunch?*

1273 Bobby to Greg and Peter: "I'm glad she's gone. I hated that
_____."

1274 Who said "Not *sunglasses* . . . shades"?

1275 Who told Peter, "If there's going to be a robbery here tonight, we'd better be ready"?

1276 Why did Bobby say, "When I get to three, I'm going to scalp her!"?

1277 Who yelled, "If you can't trust your own sister to keep a solemn promise, you can't trust anyone!"?

1278 What was Peter doing when he told Mike, "It's not working. Every time I jab, he moves. And every time I move, he jabs"?

1279 Mike: "Oh Alice, nothing's got you! With all that hardware on your head you punctured your _____!"

1280 Why did Bobby tell Carol, "Well, I can finger paint . . . and glue things"?

1281 Where was Carol when she noticed her favorite vase had been broken?

1282 Who said, "It means I have to fink on all my friends"?

1283 A goat was the mascot for which high school?

1284 What was the boys' doctor's name?

1285 Who said, "I am a little Sunflower, sunny, brave, and true. From tiny bud to blossom, I do good deeds for you"?

1286 What was the name of Peter's extremely difficult science teacher who almost flunked him?

1287 What was Jan's line in the school play *Romeo and Juliet?*

1288 Mrs. Watson (schoolteacher): "I've just learned that an error was made in scoring the _____ contest."

1289 What was Carol referring to when she told Mike, "It's part of growing up for a girl"?

1290 How did the Brady girls find out the boys were behind the "ghost" that appeared outside their bedroom window?

1291 How much did the boys receive as a reward for turning in the lost wallet Bobby found while the boys were playing football?

1292 Who was Mrs. Payne?

1293 Who said, "Poor kid. Sounds serious. Why don't you get him on the phone and see if we can stop over after practice?"

1294 Who asked, "Harvey, how about a bug sandwich?"

1295 What was Alice referring to when she said, "Sam, that's about as romantic a gift as a year's supply of chalk for their fingers"?

1296 To whom was Greg's math teacher engaged?

1297 Who said, "You brought Tiger?! He'll frighten Fluffy to death!"?

1298 Who took the dirty laundry bag, containing Carol's favorite earrings, down to the laundry room?

1299 Who was Alice referring to when she said, "Like I said, she's efficient, well organized . . . a born manager"?

1300 Who told Mike and Carol, "All the girls want to be Priscilla and all the boys want to be Indians"?

1301 To whom did Jan say, "What I want to know is what's with you . . . and Clark Tyson?"

1302 Who said, "Man on first and third with an out. The batter must . . . pour a cup of vinegar into . . . the catcher's mitt. This is the best way to hide the signals from . . . the salt and pepper. Always be sure to properly season every . . . umpire. He is not allowed to pitch or touch his finger to his . . . pot. Always remember that too many onions or too much garlic will . . . keep the shortstop away from the third baseman"?

1303 Who yelled, "Now wait a minute, you! You're talking about my sister! You start a rumor like that and I'll personally knock your head in!"?

1304 Why couldn't the original Lady Capulet play her role at the last minute?

1305 Who said, "I bet she's a heck of a good button-sewer-onner"?

1306 What was Carol referring to when she said, "Well, Marcia and Greg are going, but they're older. And, um, Jan and Peter are going too"?

1307 Who was Hank Carter?

1308 Who was Jan referring to when she told Carol, "Sue Berry said he sounded like a frog!"?

1309 Who was the cheerleader Greg photographed doing cheers during the play that lost his team the football game?

1310 Who was Connie Hutchins?

1311 Who said, "Cindy, I'm going to win this fair and square, brother or no brother"?

1312 Where was Bobby when he had his first kiss?

1313 Who read from the *TeenTime Romance* magazine, "One way to achieve a successful marriage is for the girl to marry a man who is ten to twelve years older than her"?

1314 Why did Greg say, "I know one thing I can do. I can have a man-to-man with Mr. Duncan, the park director"?

1315 What was Greg referring to when he said, "Look, it sounds to me like Bobby's telling the truth. But I'm willing to give Jerry a fair shake"?

1316 How did Bobby and Cindy get lost in the Grand Canyon?

1317 To whom did Carol warn, "No loading up you two on everything in sight. We're going to have a big lunch"?

1318 Why did Jan say, "I'm the stumble-foot of the century"?

1319 Who was Marcia referring to when she told Greg, "He may be your opposition, but he's not mine"?

1320 What was Marcia referring to when she said, "Let's look on the bright side. At least we don't have to worry about being snitched on"?

1321 What was Jan referring to when she told Marcia, "I'll have to get another one. Luckily they're not too expensive"?

1322 Who said, "Say, how would you boys like to hear how I stole the enemy code book single-handed?"

1323 Who said, "You know something, Cindy? I think your mom has a problem about discussing sex"?

1324 Who kept calling Carol's Aunt Jenny during her visit with the Bradys?

1325 Where was Greg told to keep Myron over the weekend?

1326 Who was Carol referring to when she shouted, "Mike! Where is he? He should have come up by now!"?

1327 What was Marcia referring to when she said, "Well . . . because they come from groceries and taking care of groceries is a woman's job!"?

1328 How were the Bradys able to find Jan's missing locket?

1329 Who asked, "Mom, Dad? Is there something going on around here that I should know about?"

1330 Who told Peter over the phone, "Oh, then you're the groovy-looking one who was fixing the car"?

1331 Who broke his date with Marcia after seeing her with a bruised nose?

1332 To whom did Cindy say, "See, the wicked witch has cast a spell on you. That's why you're a bullfrog"?

1333 Who was Marcia referring to when she said, "I want this telegram delivered to him personally"?

1334 How much money did Mr. Dimsdale want in advance to reserve a recording studio for Greg?

1335 How many chin-ups can Greg do?

1336 To whom did Greg say, "You showed me your secret slider!"?

1337 Why didn't Peter want to go to Lucy Winter's birthday party?

1338 Why did Alice run into the kitchen screaming, "Look on the front page!"?

1339 Who said, "Bobby? Look, I'm sorry about that 'Shrimpo' remark"?

1340 What color was the living room carpet?

1341 What was Greg referring to when he said, "Well, how do you like that? Most guys would be jumping around screaming their heads off and my kooky sister goes to sleep"?

1342 What was Cindy referring to when she said, "No. And please don't ask me who did. I'm not going to tattle on my mommy"?

1343 Mike: "Tiger, you've been accused of _____-napping and _____-snatching. How do you plead?"

1344 Who said, "Morning, Carol. Morning, Mike"?

1345 Who said, "No wonder you guys like me so much. You're pigeons and I'm a chicken"?

1346 What was Alice doing the night Mike and Carol left Greg and Marcia to baby-sit the rest of the kids?

1347 What was Marcia referring to when she told Mike and Carol, "Peter really played a dirty trick on us"?

1348 What was Mr. Delafield's profession?

1349 What was Buddy Hinton's father's name?

1350 Who said, "No false modesty. I do not believe in false modesty. I am beautiful so I say I am beautiful. You are talented, no?"

1351 Who said, "Maybe we can go steady just once a week"?

1352 Who was Elizabeth Carter?

1353 At what event was Colonel Dick Whitfield guest of honor?

1354 Greg to Peter: "A _____ has the size and shape of a monkey, man, or any old ape."

1355 Which three individuals each invited a boy to the house to ask Marcia to the school dance after her date canceled the day after she got braces?

1356 Which Brady won and lost his/her role in the school play?

1357 Who said, "Oh, I don't mind, Mrs. Brady. I'm glad it worked out this way. Arthur likes to dance and he's got two good knees"?

1358 To whom did Greg say, "I'm delivering these important designs for him right now. If I ever get there, that is"?

1359 Which act won first prize on the *Pete Stern Amateur Hour*?

1360 Name one trick the boys played on Marcia and her friends at her slumber party.

1361 What was Mike referring to when he said, "Gosh, that looks like how I sometimes feel when I get up in the morning"?

1362 Who said, "Me and the Mrs. have been saving up for this trip for years"?

1363 To whom did Alice say, "Now you two might be Mr. and Mrs. Brady. But you three are *definitely* not Greg, Peter, and Bobby"?

1364 What family outing was Marcia grounded from for sneaking out of her bedroom window in the middle of the night?

1365 Were Alice and Sam ever engaged during the original series between 1969 and 1974?

1366 Who said, "I'm stuck with two Romeos and no Juliets"?

1367 Whose birthday party was Carol's Aunt Jenny invited to while staying with the Bradys?

1368 Where did the Bradys find Myron after Jan took him?

1369 What did the boys use to make their trail while looking for the ancient burial ground in Hawaii?

1370 Who won the driving contest?

1371 How many books of Checker trading stamps did the Brady kids have all together?

1372 Why did Jan say, "This is the happiest morning of my life after the happiest night of my life"?

1373 What was the name of Mike's client played by Natalie Schafer (a.k.a. Lovey Howell)?

1374 Who said, "Greg Brady! You're even worse than Jan said! I *never* want to see you again!"?

1375 What was Doug Simpson also known as?

1376 What was Mrs. Engstrom referring to when she said, "It was nice of the children to give this *special* performance"?

1377 Who was Marcia's date at the Fillmore Junior High prom?

1378 What was the name of the song the Brady Six recorded after Greg scratched his first one when Peter's voice started to change?

1379 How did Bobby put a hole in the roof of Mike's convertible?

1380 What did the Bradys get in payment for agreeing to do the Safe soap commercial?

1381 Who asked Jan, "After giving that speech, how about being my date at the dance?"

1382 What kind of costume was Peter wearing when Arthur Owens came over to his house?

1383 Who said, "Hey Greg, you ought to keep your head sticking out. It's nice and warm out here"?

1384 What was Alice's last name?

1385 Who said, "Ghost be gone! Anti-witchcraft charm, if you ever worked, work now"?

1386 How much did Greg get for his first car from the junk man?

1387 What was Cindy referring to when she told Mike, "Peter was using the top to strain a guppy out of the fish tank"?

1388 Who said, "It's terrible. You can't even hear the words"?

1389 What was Mike's boss, Mr. Matthews's first name?

1390 Carol to Greg: "You may have invented a whole new dish. Pepperoni _____ pizza."

1391 Who said, "Okay, now team, I want you to listen to what I'm laying down. Now, Love, you're over there at the counter, see, and you're makin' with the greenery. And then, Pops, you come flippin' in and you lay this box of flakes on the little lady"?

1392 What was Cindy referring to when she asked, "Alice, if I sit in that chair, can I fib a little?"

1393 Who was George Glass?

1394 Why did Bobby drop out of the magazine subscription–selling contest?

1395 What was the name of the pizza parlor where Peter got a part-time job after Marcia fired him from the ice cream shop?

1396 Marcia: "We can spend up to ten dollars on the _____ and I was trying to decide what was the best way to use the money."

1397 Why did Mike have to use the kids' pay phone to make an important business call?

1398 Why did Greg hate Warren Mulaney?

1399 Who was Sam referring to when he said, "Nothing. I was just getting to the patio door and he ran right into your frozen leg of lamb"?

1400 What immediately followed Carol's saying, "Welcome to the family, Oliver!"?

1401 Who said, "Boy, I really learned something. One, you act your age. Two, don't try to be someone you're not. And three, you find out in advance what restaurant your parents are going to and go someplace else"?

1402 How did Peter and Bobby try to get Marcia to move out of the attic?

1403 Marcia to a surprised Greg: "So *you're* the _____!"

1404 What did Bobby capture on film that made Alice so happy?

1405 Who did Greg choose as the new head cheerleader?

1406 What was Carol referring to when she said, "Mike, what if you lose your job?"

1407 What "chores" did Bobby make Peter do after he saved Peter's life?

1408 What was Mike referring to when he said, "So much for operation bounce back"?

1409 Why did Jimmy Pakaya run away?

1410 Who said, "Tami, Buddy, I'm about to lay a new sound on you. The sound of a guy taking a walk"?

1411 Marcia: "What a groovy day on Mr. Phillips's _____."

1412 Who said, "I could have left them on that little island. We were all over it!"?

1413 Who was Miss Claret?

1414 Why did Jerry Rogers get kicked out of the big game between Fairview and Westdale?

1415 To whom did Mike say, "Hi, folks. Funny thing happened to me on the way to the market"?

1416 Who said, "Son, you with the camera. Get a picture of me reporting this"?

1417 Alice: "I got my old _____ back, Mr. Foster, and I'm never going to leave it again."

1418 What was Bobby referring to when he told Mike, "We were just going to keep them in there till you came"?

1419 On what occasion did Carol say, "And Cindy, what happened to your curls? A half hour ago I made you curls!"?

1420 Who said, "In Japan, a sip like that would be an insult to the cook! Let's hear it, Honey!"?

1421 What was the name of the neighbor's cat?

1422 Who played Professor Hubert Whitehead?

1423 What was Bobby referring to when he said, "It was the worst dream in the whole world"?

1424 What was Greg referring to when he asked, "How close was she?"

1425 What did the girls want to get with their Checker trading stamps?

1426 Who was Carol referring to when she told Mike: "I hope you learned your lesson too. The next time you have to deal with Penelope Fletcher, just do your _____ imitation."

1427 Who said, "Take my rainbow and sunlit light."

1428 Marcia: "Oh! My _____!"

1429 To whom did Marcia say, "You have to ask Daddy or you'll hurt his feelings. Mom will understand"?

1430 Who said, "Well, how about the flip side?"

1431 Greg: "If we don't use the _____ on Friday, we lose the money."

1432 What was Carol referring to when she said, "Greg, you can't pin all your hopes on one thing in life"?

1433 Who was Myrna Carter?

1434 Who said, "Suddenly I feel about as popular as the measles"?

1435 Who said, "If everyone *had* come that I invited, I may have gone on for years being a real little stinker"?

1436 What was Greg referring to when he said, "This will never work. Glue will never hold this frame together"?

1437 Who said, "I sure hope I'm small enough"?

1438 Which Brady girl slept closest to the bedroom door?

1439 Who said, "It's warm in here. Put the top down"?

1440 What was the name of the prospective buyer of the Brady house?

1441 Mike to Carol: "Another evening wasted with that hokey _____ queen."

1442 What happened when Bobby gave Cindy a new Kitty Karry-All doll?

1443 What was Carol referring to when she said, "It's amazing how quickly it went from Danish Modern to American Disaster"?

1444 What was Mike referring to when he said, "Okay, men, I want to hear the sounds of a real building being put up"?

1445 Marcia to Mike and Carol: "You know what _____ says? A girl my age is like a twenty-year-old used to be and a boy of fourteen is like twenty-two."

1446 Who said, "Boy, keeping them married sure is going to be hard work"?

1447 What was Mike referring to when he told Carol, "You know, this wouldn't have happened if you stayed off the phone"?

1448 What did Mom always say?

1449 What was Mike referring to when he said, "Boy, times sure have changed. I did the same thing when I was a kid and got suspended for a week"?

1450 Who told Peter, "The easiest way to remember things is to make up little rhymes about them. Like a vertebrate has a back that's straight"?

1451 What was Marcia referring to when she yelled, "So you've all been bribed!"?

1452 How many points did Nora Cooms score in the essay contest on Americanism?

1453 Who was Pamela Phillips?

1454 What were the kids doing in the backyard when Jan barged in and interrupted, yelling, "If I'm an only child then this is *my* backyard!"?

1455 What was the name of the show the Brady kids performed on hoping to win the hundred-dollar prize?

1456 Marcia: "Not only is this bookmark in the wrong place, but I always put my _____ back under my phone book."

1457 Who was Willie Dowrimple?

1458 Who was Greg referring to when he told the other kids, "We've spun our web, now we just have to wait for the fly"?

1459 Where was Mike presented with the "Father of the Year" award?

1460 To whom did Jan say, "Whenever Alice comes home, she's always laughing, giggling, and humming"?

1461 What was the name of Sam and Alice's mixed doubles bowling team?

1462 How did Mr. Stoner lose his wallet?

1463 To whom did Mike say, "It's the old principle of *caveat emptor*"?

1464 What was Charley referring to when he said, "Dad says some of them are pretty expensive. But seeing that you're Marcia's mother, I think I can arrange a discount"?

1465 Who said, "*You'll* never guess what happened! I got the *right* Linda!"?

1466 Who said, "Now you go first and announce me. I want to make a big entrance"?

1467 How many packs of chewing gum did Bobby win playing pool with Mike's boss?

1468 Who said, "I bet I'm the hit of Lucy's party tonight"?

1469 Where did the three Kelly boys run away to?

1470 What was Marcia doing at the time Jan's locket disappeared?

1471 What was Mr. Price referring to when he said, "Peter, I've been a teacher long enough to recognize a soft soap job"?

1472 What Shirley Temple song did Cindy sing and dance to with one of Mike's clients?

1473 Who said, "Michael, I'm afraid I'm going to have to get another architect. Good-bye. And good-bye to you, little woman"?

1474 What book did the Bradys give the Kelly boys as a gift?

1475 How did Mike get Mr. Duggan to turn his head in court?

1476 Which Brady had a surprise birthday party in his/her honor?

1477 What did Marcia mean when she said, "Well, I've still got this weekend. Maybe something will happen"?

1478 What was the name of the television show on which Bobby appeared in an ice cream eating contest?

1479 Why did Alice say, "Third prize?! What a gyp! That's the last time I ever watch that crooked channel!"?

1480 Where was Marcia when she was told, "I'm afraid you're twenty-four hours late for Davy Jones"?

1481 Why did Marcia squirt her boyfriend with whipped cream?

1482 What rumor did Greg's campaign manager want to spread about Marcia so Greg would beat her in the election for student council?

1483 Who said, "Well, we seem to be in agreement on that. What we have here is a clean dog"?

1484 How did Greg use Kathy Lawrence to get back at Marcia for going out with Warren Mulaney?

1485 Who was Mike referring to when he told Carol, "Honey, let's face it. What we have here is Frank Lloyd Wrong"?

1486 Carol and Marcia performed a song and dance from which musical?

1487 Who lay outside in the car howling in the middle of the night in a particular episode?

1488 What was Randi Petersen doing when Greg interrupted to ask where her father was?

1489 Who was the quizmaster of the *Question the Kids* television show?

1490 Marcia: "I hate_____! I hate it! I hate it!"

1491 Who was Alfred Bailey?

1492 What nickname did Tank Gates give Carol back in high school?

1493 What was the name of the air force base Mike called to report the UFO Peter and Bobby photographed?

1494 Who sent the Bradys a plaster cast from his/her broken leg?

1495 Which Brady did not attend Greg's high school graduation?

1496 What was Carol's middle name?

1497 What was Peter doing all night while Bobby was locked in the bedroom closet?

1498 Why did Cindy pretend to sprain her ankle?

1499 Why couldn't Jan be Peter's assistant in his magic act?

1500 What movie studio did the Brady family visit?

Part Three

The Answers

1 Mike and the boys.
Pilot: "The Honeymoon"

2 The letter written to the advice column *Dear Libby,* which all the Bradys were afraid was about *their* family.
Episode 1: "Dear Libby"

3 The little tiki statue Bobby found in Hawaii.
Episode 73: "Pass the Tabu"

4 Cindy's favorite doll.
Episode 3: "Kitty KarryAll Is Missing"

5 Jan.
Episode 4: "Katchoo"

6 Marcia, who had to mail her "Father of the Year" entry by midnight that night.
Episode 7: "Father of the Year"

7 Joe Namath, who had been lured to the Brady house under false pretenses.
Episode 96: "Mail Order Hero"

8 A frog, which had been left in the back seat of the car by Bobby and Peter after Greg took them to a frog-jumping contest.
Episode 89: "Greg Gets Grounded"

9 Phone.
Episode 9: "Sorry, Right Number"

10 The bottom of the Grand Canyon.
Episode 51: "The Brady Braves"

11 Greg, after both brother and sister were nominated for Student Council.
Episode 13: "Vote for Brady"

12 Greg, Peter, and Bobby, who were there to return the little tiki statue Bobby had found to the tomb of the first king.
Episode 74: "The Tiki Caves"

13 Collecting bugs.
Episode 25: "Going, Going . . . Steady"

14 She pictured the examiner in his underwear.
Episode 108: "The Driver's Seat"

15 Tiger.

General

16 Marcia.

Episode 24: "The Possible Dream"

17 Peter.

Episode 111: "Two Petes in a Pod"

18 Cindy, who had a definite lisp problem.

Episode 35: "A Fistful of Reasons"

19 Jan, because she wanted to change her image.

Episode 42: "Will the Real Jan Brady Please Stand Up?"

20 Peter.

Episode 85: "Everyone Can't Be George Washington"

21 Bobby.

Episode 105: "My Brother's Keeper"

22 Bobby's kissing her.

Episode 99: "Never Too Young"

23 Attic.

Episode 94: "A Room at the Top"

24 Cindy.

Episode 88: "The Great Earring Caper"

25 Greg, whose latest fling dumped him after he voted for another girl to be head cheerleader.

Episode 86: "Greg's Triangle"

26 Jan, who didn't know that Myron (the mouse) had gnawed its way out of the hamper.

Episode 34: "The Impractical Joker"

27 Jan, after discovering her locket was missing.

Episode 23: "Lost Locket, Found Locket"

28 Blue.

General

29 He was an architect.

General

30 Alice.

Episode 21: "The Big Sprain"

31 Marcia, who hadn't realized he was married.

Episode 84: "Love and the Older Man"

32 Greg, who had just been caught with cigarettes in his coat pocket.
Episode 41: "Where There's Smoke"

33 Jan.
Episode 66: "Jan's Aunt Jenny"

34 Blue.
General

35 Mike.
Episode 18: "To Move or Not to Move"

36 Marcia, who had been unjustly accused of drawing an unflattering picture of her English teacher.
Episode 30: "The Slumber Caper"

37 Peter, whose volcano eventually erupted all over Marcia and the snobby Booster Club she was trying to join.
Episode 75: "Today I Am a Freshman"

38 The man she had gotten into a car accident with.
Episode 70: "The Fender Benders"

39 Davy Jones.
Episode 67: "Getting Davy Jones"

40 She was jealous of her sister, who had won so many awards, while *she* hadn't won any.
Episode 55: "Her Sister's Shadow"

41 Jan, who didn't think anyone ever noticed her.
Episode 42: "Will the Real Jan Brady Please Stand Up?"

42 Bobby, who was upset after not being picked for the Glee Club.
Episode 40: "The Drummer Boy"

43 Mike, whose horoscope came true when Beebe Gallini walked into his office.
Episode 16: "Mike's Horror-Scope"

44 Orange.
General

45 The UFO the two boys were convinced they saw in the backyard.
Episode 110: "Out of This World"

46 Greg, who made him wear the mustache to appear older.
Episode 100: "Peter and the Wolf"

47 Great Grandpa Brady.

Episode 93: "You're Never Too Old"

48 Jesse James.

Episode 87: "Bobby's Hero"

49 Her and Carol, whom she had volunteered to sing and dance in the Westdale High's Family Night Frolics.

Episode 81: "The Show Must Go On"

50 Greg, who had Mike believing he wanted to be an architect because of a paper he wrote for school.

Episode 78: "Career Fever"

51 Peter, in which he padded the truth in order to make friends.

Episode 68: "The Power of the Press"

52 Greg, who bet he could do twice as many as Bobby.

Episode 65: "The Big Bet"

53 Greg, who knew she was afraid he would get hurt.

Episode 60: "Click"

54 A laundry detergent commercial.

Episode 59: "And Now a Word from Our Sponsor"

55 Sam, who had no idea Mark was in town.

Episode 48: "Alice's September Song"

56 Bobby, who was feeling sorry for himself after Cindy came home with a trophy for playing jacks.

Episode 46: "The Winner"

57 Baseball.

Episode 26: "The Dropout"

58 Movie studio.

Episode 112: "Welcome Aboard"

59 Her three newly adopted boys, who were each of a different ethnic background.

Episode 107: "Kellys' Kids"

60 People were going to be upset because Marcia was dating a guy from Fairview High's football team, Westdale's rival.

Episode 103: "Quarterback Sneak"

61 The agent (Tami Cutler) who discovered Greg while the Brady kids were auditioning for a talent contest.

Episode 98: "Adios, Johnny Bravo"

62 A silver platter.
Episode 92: "Amateur Nite"

63 Bobby, who let his position of School Safety Monitor go to his head.
Episode 79: "Law and Disorder"

64 She was a drill sergeant for the army.
Episode 69: "Sergeant Emma"

65 Peter, who had gone to a party where someone told him he was boring.
Episode 54: "The Personality Kid"

66 Greg, who promptly went out and bought a used car.
Episode 53: "The Wheeler Dealer"

67 Mike's architectural firm was involved in shutting down the local park to build a new county courthouse in its place.
Episode 47: "Double Parked"

68 Marcia, in an attempt to prove she could do anything that boys could do.
Episode 44: "The Liberation of Marcia Brady"

69 The article she wrote for *Tomorrow's Woman* magazine about her marriage and six kids.
Episode 39: "Tell It Like It Is"

70 Greg, who got the whole Brady family involved in its production.
Episode 29: "The Un-Underground Movie"

71 Peter, whose tale of heroism began to bore everyone around him.
Episode 22: "The Hero"

72 The measles.
Episode 10: "Is There a Doctor in the House?"

73 Sam, after Bobby and Oliver began questioning her about Sam's character when they began suspecting he was a double agent.
Episode 115: "Top Secret"

74 Greg, who was involved in stealing a rival high school's mascot as an act of revenge.
Episode 101: "Getting Greg's Goat"

75 Greg, who had almost gotten into an accident while looking at his new record album and driving at the same time.
Episode 89: "Greg Gets Grounded"

76 Jan, who felt she didn't have any privacy.
Episode 80: "Jan, the Only Child"

77 Marcia, who was nominated *after* she had helped the class dweeb (who had been nominated by her classmates as a joke) transform into a breathtaking beauty.
Episode 71: "My Fair Opponent"

78 Cindy, who was fed up with being the youngest.
Episode 67: "Cindy Brady, Lady"

79 Greg, who had just been turned away by a recording studio because he didn't have enough money to record his new song.
Episode 64: "Dough Re Mi"

80 Peter.
Episode 58: "The Private Ear"

81 A deserted old ghost town.
Episode 49: "Ghost Town USA"

82 Marcia, who was also running for Student Council.
Episode 13: "Vote for Brady"

83 Blue.
General

84 Bobby, before being kissed by Millicent.
Episode 99: "Never Too Young"

85 Greg.
Episode 34: "The Impractical Joker"

86 Bobby, who didn't have time to spit out the toothpaste when Greg told him to get in bed while the family re-enacted the events that led up to the disappearance of Jan's locket.
Episode 23: "Lost Locket, Found Locket"

87 Greg, after using the hair tonic he bought from Bobby.
Episode 116: "The Hair-Brained Scheme"

88 His biological mother's picture, just before Mike and Carol's wedding.
Pilot: "The Honeymoon"

89 Mike, after he and Carol switched roles for a day.
Episode 8: "The Grass Is Always Greener"

90 Cindy, practicing her Ss.
Episode 35: "A Fistful of Reasons"

91 On the first floor by the laundry room.
General

92 Greg.
Episode 33: "Call Me Irresponsible"

93 Tiger, who had been running off with whatever he could get his teeth into.
Episode 32: "The Tattletale"

94 The kids heard them sneaking around out back, got scared, and called the police.
Episode 27: "The Baby-sitters"

95 Phone.
Episode 9: "Sorry, Right Number"

96 Bobby.
Episode 116: "The Hair-Brained Scheme"

97 Cindy, who was convinced that something was going on that involved her.
Episode 113: "The Snooperstar"

98 Amusement park.
Episode 102: "The Cincinnati Kids"

99 Cindy.
Episode 95: "Snow White and the Seven Bradys"

100 Marcia.
General

101 Carol.
Episode 77: "Fright Night"

102 Bobby, giving Peter the old "I told you so" bit after Peter broke Mom's favorite vase.
Episode 31: "Confessions, Confessions"

103 Peter and Bobby.
General

104 Greg.
Episode 44: "The Liberation of Marcia Brady"

105 So she could sing at church.
Episode 15: "The Voice of Christmas"

106 Tiger, the boys' dog.
Pilot: "The Honeymoon"

107 Alice.
Episode 32: "The Tattletale"

108 Sam, referring to the Meat Cutter's Ball, which Alice couldn't attend because she was laid up in bed with a sprained ankle.
Episode 21: "The Big Sprain"

109 Cindy.
General

110 Her first slumber party.
Episode 30: "The Slumber Caper"

111 Greg, after giving him a part-time job with his architectural firm.
Episode 33: "Call Me Irresponsible"

112 Cindy.
Episode 37: "Coming Out Party"

113 A brunette wig.
Episode 42: "Will the Real Jan Brady Please Stand Up?"

114 Greg.
Episode 17: "The Undergraduate"

115 Sam.
General

116 A lisp.
General

117 Marcia, while watching her try to brush her teeth after getting braces.
Episode 20: "Brace Yourself"

118 Jan.
General

119 All of the kids.
Episode 44: "Is There a Doctor in the House?"

120 Hawaii.
Episode 72: "Hawaii Bound"

121 Jan, who would soon find out she needed glasses.
Episode 61: "The Not-So-Rose-Colored Glasses"

122 Bobby and Cindy, who were out to set a world's teeter-tottering record.
Episode 56: "The Teeter-Totter Caper"

123 Cindy, after seeing a magician make a lady disappear into the darkness.
Episode 45: "Lights Out"

124 Bobby, who was attempting to climb up to a treehouse.
Episode 36: "What Goes Up . . . "

125 The wallet Bobby found in an old lot.
Episode 28: "The Treasure of Sierra Avenue"

126 Marcia.
Episode 24: "The Possible Dream"

127 The reward he was offering to anyone who found Tiger, their lost dog.
Episode 19: "Tiger! Tiger!"

128 Bobby, after Cindy's favorite doll was discovered missing, minutes after Bobby had been in the room.
Episode 3: "Kitty KarryAll Is Missing"

129 Alice, referring to Mike as Carol asked her if she thought Mike could have written the letter to "Dear Libby" about a terrible family situation.
Episode 1: "Dear Libby"

130 Mike, after receiving a pool table with no card attached.
Episode 114: "The Hustler"

131 Jan.
Episode 109: "Miss Popularity"

132 Marcia, after Peter slacked off at the ice cream parlor where Marcia was the manager.
Episode 104: "Marcia Gets Creamed"

133 Sam, in a fit of rage.
Episode 97: "The Elopement"

134 Peter, who had just gotten a job fixing bikes at a bike store.
Episode 91: "How to Succeed in Business"

135 Alice, as she told Carol that she was leaving the Bradys.
Episode 83: "Goodbye, Alice, Hello"

136 Bobby, who, after being told to stay off the ladder, climbed up anyway and nearly got killed when the ladder fell.
Episode 62: "Little Big Man"

137 Juliet.
Episode 52: "Juliet Is the Sun"

138 Carol's favorite vase, after water leaked all over the dinner table.
Episode 31: "Confessions, Confessions"

139 The guitar.
General

140 His den looked like a scene from *Love American Style* when Mike told Greg he could turn it into a bedroom.
Episode 43: "Our Son, the Man"

141 Because Cindy was going to have her tonsils taken out.
Episode 37: "Coming Out Party"

142 Bobby.
General

143 Carol.
Episode 15: "The Voice of Christmas"

144 Alice, to Mike and Carol, who were in disagreement over whose job was harder.
Episode 8: "The Grass Is Always Greener"

145 Alice, who was making up an excuse to leave the Bradys after feeling like she wasn't needed anymore.
Episode 6: "Alice Doesn't Live Here Anymore"

146 They brought the entire family along, including Alice.
Pilot: "The Honeymoon"

147 Bobby, comparing sports to girls.
Episode 99: "Never Too Young"

148 Peter, after meeting his double at school.
Episode 111: "Two Petes in a Pod"

149 A bug.
Episode 25: "Going, Going . . . Steady"

150 Checkers.
General

151 Mike and Carol deciding that Greg could move his room into the attic instead of Marcia.
Episode 94: "A Room at the Top"

152 Because Carol had just announced to the kids that Greg and Marcia would be baby-sitting that night.
Episode 27: "The Baby-sitters"

153 Marcia doodled the doodle, then a friend gave it the title after Marcia left it sitting on her desk.
Episode 30: "The Slumber Caper"

154 Marcia, after Greg began complaining that there were too many beauty products cluttering up their bathroom.
Episode 2: "A Clubhouse Is Not a Home"

155 Peter.
General

156 Jan, after seeing a picture of her great aunt Jenny who looked just like Jan at her age.
Episode 66: "Jan's Aunt Jenny"

157 Cindy, referring to the kids at school.
Episode 35: "A Fistful of Reasons"

158 He had Greg hide in the bushes in her backyard and feed him romantic lines while he stood outside Kerry's window.
Episode 67: "Cyrano De Brady"

159 Cindy, after learning her lesson about tattling.
Episode 32: "The Tattletale"

160 Cindy, after he promised he would give Carol her voice back in time for Christmas.
Episode 15: "The Voice of Christmas"

161 Peter, who had just bought a detective kit.
Episode 88: "The Great Earring Caper"

162 Choosing *another* girl to be the new head cheerleader.
Episode 86: "Greg's Triangle"

163 Marcia, fearing that she wouldn't be popular.
Episode 75: "Today I Am a Freshman"

164 Carol, who had been in a car accident.
Episode 70: "The Fender Benders"

165 Tiger, the boys' dog, chasing Fluffy, the girls' cat.
Pilot: "The Honeymoon"

166 Bobby, after the two kids finished watching Cinderella on TV.
Episode 14: "Every Boy Does It Once"

167 Marcia.
Episode 44: "The Liberation of Marcia Brady"

168 Peter, trying to avoid a physical fight with his classmate who had been picking on Cindy.
Episode 35: "A Fistful of Reasons"

169 Bobby, who hid the fact that he'd been exposed to the mumps after kissing a girl.
Episode 99: "Never Too Young"

170 Davy Jones, who she wanted to ask to sing at her junior high school prom.
Episode 63: "Getting Davy Jones"

171 Jan, who thought she had won her school's essay contest on Americanism.
Episode 55: "Her Sister's Shadow"

172 Jan, who thought wearing a wig might get her noticed more.
Episode 42: "Will the Real Jan Brady Please Stand Up?"

173 Because he was a member of the school Glee Club.
Episode 40: "The Drummer Boy"

174 Marcia, who was referring to Harvey Klinger.
Episode 25: "Going, Going . . . Steady"

175 Mike.
General

176 Carol, who was worried that Mike's horoscope would come true.
Episode 16: "Mike's Horror-Scope"

177 Because she got the role of the Fairy Princess in her school play.
Episode 5: "Eenie, Meenie, Mommy, Daddy"

178 The right side.
General

179 Greg, who was desperately looking for a date for his date's cousin.
Episode 100: "Peter and the Wolf"

180 Great Grandpa Brady.
Episode 93: "You're Never Too Old"

181 Bobby, to Cindy, discussing stepmothers after watching *Cinderella* on TV.
Episode 14: "Every Boy Does It Once"

182 Alice, talking to the exterminator after seeing Greg's mouse (she didn't know it was his) running around the house.
Episode 34: "The Impractical Joker"

183 Carol, after she and Mike switched roles for the day.
Episode 8: "The Grass Is Always Greener"

184 Bobby, who claimed Jesse James was his hero.
Episode 87: "Bobby's Hero"

185 Carol.
Episode 81: "The Show Must Go On"

186 Greg, who was having a hard time telling Mike he didn't want to be an architect.
Episode 78: "Career Fever"

187 Peter, who wrote a column for his school newspaper.
Episode 68: "The Power of the Press"

188 A bruise.
Episode 60: "Click"

189 A dog.
General

190 Skyrockets.
Episode 99: "Never Too Young"

191 To get the kids.
Pilot: "The Honeymoon"

192 Mike, to Carol, arguing that there are certain things that boys and girls don't do with each other.
Episode 2: "A Clubhouse Is Not a Home"

193 Marcia, after telling Mike and Greg she didn't want to be a Frontier Scout after all.
Episode 44: "The Liberation of Marcia Brady"

194 Greg.
Episode 41: "Where There's Smoke"

195 Alice, to Mike who commented on what he thought was her boyfriend's attempt at a love letter, actually written by Greg to someone else.
Episode 17: "The Undergraduate"

196 Greg.
General

197 She wanted to see which laundry detergent was better.
Episode 59: "And Now a Word from Our Sponsors"

198 Alice's old high school flame who came back to town to sweep her off her feet.
Episode 48: "Alice's September Song"

199 Bobby, who was the only Brady without a trophy.
Episode 46: "The Winner"

200 Peter, as he tried to reason with Buddy about teasing Cindy.
Episode 35: "A Fistful of Reasons"

201 Greg, who was convinced he was going to be a baseball star one day.
Episode 26: "The Dropout"

202 The girls had won the house of cards contest against the boys, as well as all the Checker trading stamp books.
Episode 11: "54-40 and Fight"

203 Jan, who stayed home from school because of uncontrollable sneezing.
Episode 4: "Katchoo"

204 Cousin Oliver, who moved in with the Bradys' during their last season.
Episode 112: "Welcome Aboard"

205 Playbook.
Episode 103: "Quarterback Sneak"

206 Greg.
Episode 98: "Adios, Johnny Bravo"

207 Carol.
General

208 Tiger, their lost dog.
Episode 19: "Tiger! Tiger!"

209 Carol and Cindy.
Episode 37: "Coming Out Party"

210 He was in love with his math teacher.
Episode 17: "The Undergraduate"

211 Jan was wearing a brunette wig.
Episode 42: "Will the Real Jan Brady Please Stand Up?"

212 The silver platter the kids bought for Mike and Carol's anniversary gift.
Episode 92: "Amateur Nite"

213 A man.
Episode 84: "Love and the Older Man"

214 Bobby, who had just been made a school safety monitor.
Episode 79: "Law and Disorder"

215 Alice's cousin Emma, who had been staying with the Bradys, would be leaving and there would be no more 0600-hour calisthenics, white glove tests, or quarters inspections.
Episode 69: "Sergeant Emma"

216 Greg's looking for a used car.
Episode 53: "The Wheeler Dealer"

217 The kids' local playground, Woodland Park.
Episode 47: "Double Parked"

218 She had just finished writing her article about the family for *Tomorrow's Woman* magazine.
Episode 39: "Tell It Like It Is"

219 Because Greg was making a movie for a history class project.
Episode 29: "The Un-Underground Movie"

220 Alice.
General

221 Mike's den, where she secretly worked on her entry for the "Father of the Year" contest.
Episode 7: "Father of the Year"

222 Cousin Oliver, who, like Bobby, thought Sam was a double agent working against Mike and the FBI.
Episode 115: "Top Secret"

223 Jan, who had just dropped out of her ballet class because she was a klutz.
Episode 106: "Try, Try Again"

224 The rival high school's goat mascot.
Episode 101: "Getting Greg's Goat"

225 Joe Namath, who Bobby had been desperately trying to meet.
Episode 96: "Mail Order Hero"

226 Greg, who claimed that when his parents told him he couldn't drive the car for a week, they meant only *their* car, not any other car.
Episode 89: "Greg Gets Grounded"

227 The rest of the kids wanted to see Cindy fail the *Question the Kids* television game show.
Episode 82: "You Can't Win 'Em All"

228 Jan, who said she wished she were an only child.
Episode 80: "Jan, the Only Child"

229 She would be running against the class dweeb who had been nominated as a joke.
Episode 71: "My Fair Opponent"

230 Cindy, who was tired of being called the baby of the family.
Episode 67: "Cindy Brady, Lady"

231 The song he had written and wanted to record.
Episode 64: "Dough Re Mi"

232 Peter, who had been taping everyone's private conversations and getting them in trouble.
Episode 58: "The Private Ear"

233 The Grand Canyon.
Episode 49: "Ghost Town USA"

234 To get rid of her freckles.
Episode 38: "The Not-So-Ugly Duckling"

235 The postman.
Episode 32: "The Tattletale"

236 Mike, in an effort to teach Bobby about strangers.
Episode 27: "The Baby-sitters"

237 The mysterious little locket she received in the mail.
Episode 23: "Lost Locket, Found Locket"

238 Phone.
Episode 9: "Sorry, Right Number"

239 Alice, discussing with Mike and Carol what to do about bickering children.
Episode 2: "A Clubhouse Is Not a Home"

240 Marcia wrote it in her diary to teach Cindy a lesson for snooping.
Episode 113: "The Snooperstar"

241 Driver's license exam.
Episode 108: "The Driver's Seat"

242 Marcia.
Episode 90: "The Subject Was Noses"

243 The boys, who bet they could stay up in the attic all night.
Episode 77: "Fright Night"

244 To check up on a construction site for Mike's company.
Episode 72: "Hawaii Bound"

245 Jan.
Episode 61: "The Not-So-Rose-Colored Glasses"

246 Teeter-tottering.
Episode 56: "The Teeter-Totter Caper"

247 Cindy, who kept getting up to turn the light on each time Marcia got up to turn it off.
Episode 45: "Lights Out"

248 Greg, who had just been asked to join a buddy's band.
Episode 41: "Where There's Smoke"

249 Bobby, who was on his way up to a treehouse club to get sworn in as a member.
Episode 36: "What Goes Up . . . "

250 The lost wallet Bobby found.
Episode 28: "The Treasure of Sierra Avenue"

251 A used bookstore.
Episode 24: "The Possible Dream"

252 She had sprained her ankle.
Episode 21: "The Big Sprain"

253 Cindy's favorite doll, which disappeared shortly after Bobby was making fun of it.
Episode 3: "Kitty KarryAll Is Missing"

254 Bobby.
Episode 114: "The Hustler"

255 Jan, who despite being nominated "Most Popular Girl," had just lost all her friends.

Episode 109: "Miss Popularity"

256 Peter, who she had just fired from Haskell's Ice Cream Hut where Marcia was day manager.

Episode 104: "Marcia Gets Creamed"

257 Peter, who had just lost his job as a bike repairman.

Episode 91: "How to Succeed in Business"

258 Alice, who packed up and left after the kids had all given her the cold shoulder.

Episode 83: "Goodbye, Alice, Hello"

259 Bobby, who was particularly sensitive about his height.

Episode 62: "Little Big Man"

260 Marcia.

Episode 52: "Juliet Is the Sun"

261 Greg, who now as a freshman in high school, thought he was too old for campouts.

Episode 43; "Our Son, the Man"

262 Tonsils.

Episode 37: "Coming Out Party"

263 A picture Marcia had drawn and signed, which a classmate had found and entitled "Mrs. Denton: A Hippopotamus."

Episode 30: "The Slumber Caper"

264 Mike, trying to help Marcia earn her cooking badge.

Episode 8: "The Grass Is Always Greener"

265 Alice, who lied about having to go live with a sick aunt because she didn't think the Bradys needed her anymore.

Episode 6: "Alice Doesn't Live Here Anymore"

266 Mike, the morning of his wedding.

Pilot: "The Honeymoon"

267 Me.

Episode 111: "Two Petes in a Pod"

268 Peter, whose life he had just saved.

Episode 105: "My Brother's Keeper"

269 He thought he had been exposed to the mumps after kissing a girl who thought *she* had them.

Episode 99: "Never Too Young"

270 Peter, who had a crush on Jan's pretty friend.
Episode 76: "Cyrano De Brady"

271 Marcia, who faked sick on her first day of high school.
Episode 75: "Today I Am a Freshman"

272 Carol's car accident.
Episode 70: "The Fender Benders"

273 Jan, who felt as though she was in Marcia's shadow.
Episode 55: "Her Sister's Shadow"

274 Peter, Jan, or Cindy.
Episode 40: "The Drummer Boy"

275 Beebe Gallini, Mike's cosmetic queen client.
Episode 16: "Mike's Horror-Scope"

276 Cindy, who was practicing for her role as the Fairy Princess.
Episode 5: "Eenie, Meenie, Mommy, Daddy"

277 The left side.
General

278 UFO.
Episode 110: "Out of This World"

279 He was telling Peter how to act on their double date in which Peter was supposed to be older than he really was.
Episode 100: "Peter and the Wolf"

280 Great Grandma Hutchins.
Episode 93: "You're Never Too Old"

281 Coffee.
General

282 Jan, referring to Greg's mouse.
Episode 34: "The Impractical Joker"

283 Greg, who was having a hard time telling Mike he didn't want to be an architect.
Episode 78: "Career Fever"

284 Bobby.
Episode 60: "Click"

285 Laundry washed with two different detergents.
Episode 59: "And Now a Word from Our Sponsors"

286 Mark Millard, Alice's old high school flame, who came to town to sweep her off her feet and steal all her money.
Episode 48: "Alice's September Song"

287 Bobby, in an effort to win a trophy.
Episode 46: "The Winner"

288 Cindy, after practicing her Ss.
Episode 35: "A Fistful of Reasons"

289 By playing ball in the house.
Episode 31: "Confessions, Confessions"

290 Greg, who wanted to drop out of school to play ball.
Episode 26: "The Dropout"

291 Bobby, to Greg who didn't seem very impressed that Bobby did five chin-ups.
Episode 65: "The Big Bet"

292 That person and their entire party got to appear in a Marathon Studio movie.
Episode 112: "Welcome Aboard"

293 Marcia, who succumbed to his charms instantaneously.
Episode 103: "Quarterback Sneak"

294 Greg.
Episode 98: "Adios, Johnny Bravo"

295 The kids couldn't afford the engraving, which Jan had done behind their backs.
Episode 92: "Amateur Nite"

296 Her gorgeous new dentist, Dr. Stanley Vogel.
Episode 84: "Love and the Older Man"

297 Marcia, after being falsely accused of drawing a caricature of her English teacher.
Episode 30: "The Slumber Caper"

298 He fixed bikes.
Episode 91: "How To Succeed in Business"

299 Greg, after he told Marcia he had no idea how Mike and Carol could have found out.
Episode 41: "Where There's Smoke"

300 Bobby, to Cindy, who he had just caught running through the halls at school.
Episode 79: "Law and Disorder"

301 Peter, who had been told by a friend that he had no personality.
Episode 54: "The Personality Kid"

302 His old car.
Episode 53: "The Wheeler Dealer"

303 His architectural firm was building a new county courthouse on the park site.
Episode: 47: "Double Parked"

304 Carol, who had just written a story about her marriage and kids for *Tomorrow's Woman* magazine.
Episode 39: "Tell It Like It Is"

305 In the backyard.
Episode 29: "The Un-Underground Movie"

306 Peter, who was featured as a hero by the newspaper for saving a little girl's life at a local toy store.
Episode 22: "The Hero"

307 Mike, to Marcia, who got upset just before going to bed.
Episode 7: "Father of the Year"

308 They thought the two men were spies working against Mike and the FBI.
Episode 115: "Top Secret"

309 Jan, who was just feeling sorry for herself again.
Episode 106: "Try, Try Again"

310 Greg, who claimed he could live by exact words.
Episode 89: "Greg Gets Grounded"

311 Greg, who was about to hide in the bushes and feed Peter romantic lines while he stood outside a girl's window.
Episode 76: "Cyrano De Brady"

312 Cindy, who was tired of being the youngest.
Episode 67: "Cindy Brady, Lady"

313 The Brady Six.
Episode 64: "Dough Re Mi"

314 In an old jail cell at the deserted old ghost town where they made camp for the night.
Episode 49: "Ghost Town USA"

315 Jan, who made up an imaginary boyfriend so her family wouldn't think she was a loser.
Episode 38: "The Not-So-Ugly Duckling"

316 Underwear.
Episode 108: "The Driver's Seat"

317 The play *Snow White and the Seven Dwarfs*, which the Bradys had planned to put on to raise money to buy Cindy's retiring teacher a gift.
Episode 95: "Snow White and the Seven Bradys"

318 She had just been hit in the nose with a football.
Episode 90: "The Subject Was Noses"

319 Don Ho.
Episode 72: "Hawaii Bound"

320 Jan, who would later find out that she needed glasses.
Episode 61: "The Not-So-Rose-Colored Glasses"

321 Teeter-tottering.
Episode 56: "The Teeter-Totter Caper"

322 Bobby, who insisted on going along on Greg's date to the drive-in after winning a bet with him.
Episode 65: "The Big Bet"

323 Greg, who had been caught smoking.
Episode 41: "Where There's Smoke"

324 Bobby, who, despite a sprained ankle, chased his parakeet down the stairs.
Episode 36: "What Goes Up . . . "

325 Her diary.
Episode 24: "The Possible Dream"

326 Bobby, who was just about to go on mock trial for allegedly stealing Cindy's favorite doll, Kitty KarryAll.
Episode 3: "Kitty KarryAll Is Missing"

327 Bobby.
Episode 114: "The Hustler"

328 She made them all a bunch of promises to get elected, but didn't keep any of them.
Episode 109: "Miss Popularity"

329 Alice, who walked out on him because he wanted to buy Alice's cousin Clara *His and Hers* bowling balls for a wedding gift.
Episode 97: "The Elopement"

330 Alice, after leaving the Bradys.
Episode 83: "Hello, Alice, Goodbye"

331 Bobby.
Episode 62: "Little Big Man"

332 She wasn't wearing her glasses.
Episode 61: "The Not-So-Rose-Colored Glasses"

333 Peter, who decided to throw himself a party for being a hero.
Episode 22: "The Hero"

334 Peter, whose voice was changing.
Episode 64: "Dough Re Mi"

335 Egg.
Episode 108: "The Driver's Seat"

336 Don Ho.
Episode 72: "Hawaii Bound"

337 Cindy, after she got over her fear of the dark.
Episode 45: "Lights Out"

338 Tiger, who also took Cindy's favorite doll as well as a few other odds and ends.
Episode 3: "Kitty KarryAll Is Missing"

339 Myron, his science project (a mouse), which he brought home from school.
Episode 34: "The Impractical Joker"

340 Bobby, while having the old "Man to Man" with Mike.
Episode 99: "Never Too Young"

341 Marcia, who couldn't understand why she got the lead role in the school play.
Episode 52: "Juliet Is the Sun"

342 Greg, who thought he was too old for family campouts and too mature to share a bedroom with two kid brothers.
Episode 43: "Our Son, the Man"

343 Carol and Cindy's return from the hospital after having their tonsils out.
Episode 37: "Coming Out Party"

344 Cindy, who asked him to give Carol her voice back in time to sing Christmas morning.
Episode 15: "The Voice of Christmas"

345 Bobby, who was chased in there by an angry Peter.
Episode 105: "My Brother's Keeper"

346 Marcia, who was upset over Mike and Carol's decision to let Greg have the attic for his bedroom.
Episode 94: "A Room at the Top"

347 Her favorite pair of earrings.
Episode 88: "The Great Earring Caper"

348 One of the contestants was Marcia and another was his new girlfriend.
Episode 86: "Greg's Triangle"

349 Marcia, who joined every club she could when she got to high school.
Episode: 75: "Today I Am a Freshman"

350 Cindy, who was a witness to Carol's car accident.
Episode 70: "The Fender Benders"

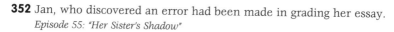

351 Davy Jones, who unexpectedly appeared at the Brady doorstep.
Episode 63: "Getting Davy Jones"

352 Jan, who discovered an error had been made in grading her essay.
Episode 55: "Her Sister's Shadow"

353 A curly wig.
Episode 42: "Will the Real Jan Brady Please Stand Up?"

354 Bobby, who was really bad.
Episode 40: "The Drummer Boy"

355 Cindy, who was trying to decide who to bring to the school play.
Episode 5: "Eenie, Meenie, Mommy, Daddy"

356 Greg, for whom Peter's love interest fell head over heels.
Episode 76: "Cyrano De Brady"

357 Peter's voice started to change throughout the song.
Episode 64: "Dough Re Mi"

358 The little tiki statue Bobby found in Hawaii.
Episode 73: "Pass the Tabu"

359 Cindy, who had been afraid to go inside Peter's disappearing box he used in his magic act.
Episode 45: "Lights Out"

360 Desi Arnaz Jr.
Episode 24: "The Possible Dream"

361 In bed, while the family was vacationing in Hawaii.
Episode 73: "Pass the Tabu"

362 Greg had turned it into his new bachelor pad.
Episode 43: "Our Son, the Man"

Part III

363 Greg and Carol.

General

364 Tiger, the family dog.

Episode 19: "Tiger! Tiger!"

365 Alice, who had been a middle child herself and thought it might make Jan feel like she was someone special.

Episode 23: "Lost Locket, Found Locket"

366 His and Carol's wedding.

Pilot: "The Honeymoon"

367 Hair tonic.

Episode 116: "The Hair-Brained Scheme"

368 Carol, who was visiting her sick Aunt Mary.

Episode 21: "The Big Sprain"

369 Ann B. Davis (Alice).

Episode 69: "Sergeant Emma"

370 Greg, as she was withdrawing from the election for student council.

Episode 13: "Vote for Brady"

371 Marcia, after she and Mike decided to switch roles for a day.

Episode 8: "The Grass Is Always Greener"

372 Her Great Aunt Jenny who once looked just like Jan when she was her age.

Episode 66: "Jan's Aunt Jenny"

373 He was a butcher.

General

374 Mike, referring to an act the two of them would do at the Westdale High Family Night Frolics.

Episode 81: "The Show Must Go On"

375 Her secret admirer, who was actually Bobby, disguising his voice, trying to make her feel older and more desirable.

Episode 76: "Cindy Brady, Lady"

376 The script for the soap commercial the Bradys were supposed to be in.

Episode 59: "And Now a Word from Our Sponsor"

377 Bobby.

Episode 46: "The Winner"

378 Baseball, after he bombed out on the pitcher's mound.

Episode 26: "The Dropout"

379 Greg, who decided not to go to college.

Episode 98: "Adios, Johnny Bravo"

380 Bobby and Cindy, in an attempt to borrow $56.23 to pay for the engraving on the silver platter the kids had bought for Mike and Carol's anniversary.
Episode 92: "Amateur Nite"

381 Her dentist, Dr. Vogel.
Episode 84: "Love and the Older Man"

382 Bobby, who was asked by a friend to help get her cat out of an old abandoned building.
Episode 79: "Law and Disorder"

383 To do early morning calisthenics, room inspections, and white glove tests.
Episode 69: "Sergeant Emma"

384 To a drive-in movie, where Bobby made a pest of himself.
Episode 65: "The Big Bet"

385 Peter, except nobody came because all his friends were sick of hearing his tale of heroism.
Episode 22: "The Hero"

386 Peter's, which caused problems for Greg and the rest of the kids who were about to record a song Greg had just written.
Episode 64: "Dough Re Mi"

387 Mike, after the boys began complaining about having to live with three new sisters.
Episode 2: "A Clubhouse Is Not a Home"

388 Desi Arnaz Jr., who dropped by the Brady house to see Marcia when he found out she had lost her diary containing her feelings about him.
Episode 24: "The Possible Dream"

389 The Kitty KarryAll doll Bobby bought for Cindy to replace the one she accused him of stealing, even though he didn't.
Episode 3: "Kitty KarryAll Is Missing"

390 Peter, who had just seen an old Bogie movie on TV.
Episode 54: "The Personality Kid"

391 Almost selling the lemon of a car *he* had bought from someone else.
Episode 53: "The Wheeler Dealer"

392 Sam, to his landlord, who Bobby and Cousin Oliver thought were trying to steal top-secret government plans from Mike and the FBI.
Episode 115: "Top Secret"

393 Jan, who had brought a painting she'd been working on to use as a prop in her audition for a school play.
Episode 106: "Try, Try Again"

394 Greg, who had been caught harboring a kidnapped goat.
Episode 101: "Getting Greg's Goat"

395 Alice, who decided to leave the Bradys after she felt she wasn't needed anymore.
Episode 6: "Alice Doesn't Live Here Anymore"

396 Mother.
Episode 8: "The Grass Is Always Greener"

397 Cindy, who appeared on the *Question the Kids* television game show.
Episode 82: "You Can't Win 'Em All"

398 Cindy, who pretended to be very mature for her first date.
Episode 67: "Cindy Brady, Lady"

399 Cindy, after Bobby accused her of not being a lady.
Episode 11: "54-40 and Fight"

400 Jan, who had a crush on Clark.
Episode 38: "The Not-So-Ugly Duckling"

401 He got cut off after he couldn't find anymore dimes to pay for the call.
Episode 9: "Sorry, Right Number"

402 Because Carol had laryngitis and wouldn't be able to sing at church.
Episode 15: "The Voice of Christmas"

403 At her and Mike's wedding.
Pilot: "The Honeymoon"

404 He had just beaten Greg in the chin-up contest.
Episode 65: "The Big Bet"

405 She was too nervous.
Episode 108: The Driver's Seat"

406 Bobby, in an attempt to explain to Alice why he thought Carol didn't love him.
Episode 14: "Every Boy Does It Once"

407 Peter, referring to his voice changing just when the kids were about to record Greg's song.
Episode 64: "Dough Re Mi"

408 Bobby bought Cindy a new doll to replace the one she accused him of stealing.
Episode 3: "Kitty KarryAll Is Missing"

409 Greg, who felt he was too old to be sharing a bedroom with Peter and Bobby.
Episode 43: "Our Son, the Man"

410 Mike's important architectural plans, which Jan lost after getting her cylinder mixed up with Mike's.
Episode 102: "The Cincinnati Kids"

411 Marcia.
Episode 90: "The Subject Was Noses"

412 Alice, who claimed that nothing scared her.
Episode 77: "Fright Night"

413 Believing Greg when he said the cigarettes, which had fallen out of his coat pocket, were not his.
Episode 41: "Where There's Smoke"

414 A trampoline.
Episode 36: "What Goes Up . . . "

415 To thank them and give them a reward for turning in his lost wallet.
Episode 28: "The Treasure of Sierra Avenue"

416 Alice, after the whole family was convinced that she and Sam had eloped.
Episode 97: "The Elopement"

417 Peter getting fired from his first job at Mr. Martinelli's Bike Shop.
Episode 91: "How to Succeed in Business"

418 Alice, who made the whole story up as an excuse to leave the Bradys after getting the cold shoulder from the kids.
Episode 83: "Goodbye, Alice, Hello"

419 Bobby, who was just small enough to squeeze out the window of the meat locker at Sam's butcher shop, where he and Greg were locked in.
Episode 62: "Little Big Man"

420 *Romeo and Juliet.*
Episode 52: "Juliet Is the Sun"

421 The little tiki statue he gave Greg to wear while surfing in a competition in Hawaii.
Episode 73: "Pass The Tabu"

422 Cindy, after overhearing Carol talking to Mike on the phone about wedding day jitters.
Pilot: "The Honeymoon"

423 Peter, whose voice was changing just as the Brady kids were about to record the song Greg wrote.
Episode 64: "Dough Re Mi"

424 He snuck out of the secret door of Peter's disappearing cabinet trick and didn't reappear until hours later.
Episode 45: "Lights Out"

425 Marcia.
Episode 76: "Cyrano De Brady"

426 A new Kitty KarryAll doll to replace the one Cindy was missing.
Episode 3: "Kitty KarryAll Is Missing"

427 Hawaii, taking a hula lesson with Carol and the girls.
Episode 72: "Hawaii Bound"

428 Peter, who had just discovered his double at school.
Episode 111: "Two Petes in a Pod"

429 Marcia.
Episode 86: "Greg's Triangle"

430 Marcia, who signed up for every club in high school, just to be popular.
Episode 75: "Today I Am a Freshman"

431 Carol, explaining to Mike how she got into a car accident.
Episode 70: "The Fender Benders"

432 Davy Jones.
Episode 63: "Getting Davy Jones"

433 Peter, who had been teased by his teammates for belonging to the Glee Club.
Episode 40: "The Drummer Boy"

434 Bobby, as he shared his fears about being a stepchild.
Episode 14: "Every Boy Does It Once"

435 Jan, making up a new boyfriend so her family wouldn't think she was a loser.
Episode 38: "The Not-So-Ugly Duckling"

436 Santa Claus, after asking him to bring Carol's voice back in time for Christmas.
Episode 15: "The Voice of Christmas"

437 Alice, to Mike after he commented on hearing bells in his sleep.
Episode 10: "Is There a Doctor in the House?"

438 Jan's locket.
Episode 23: "Lost Locket, Found Locket"

439 Mike, trying to convince Carol that his job was harder than hers.
Episode 8: "The Grass Is Always Greener"

440 Because she had a lisp.
Episode 35: "A Fistful of Reasons"

441 Bobby, after Greg and Peter passed up a game of hoops to go out with some girls.
Episode 99: "Never Too Young"

442 A mutt.
General

443 Greg.
General

444 Bobby, in an attempt to make Cindy feel older and more desirable.
Episode 67: "Cindy Brady, Lady"

445 Marcia's first slumber party.
Episode 30: "The Slumber Caper"

446 Carol, who came home smelling like fish while Mike came home smelling like perfume.
Episode 16: "Mike's Horror-Scope"

447 Cindy, who just found out that due to the number of children appearing on stage that night, she was allowed to invite only one parent to see her perform as the Fairy Princess.
Episode 5: "Eenie, Meenie, Mommy, Daddy"

448 Greg didn't want his date to know that he was setting her cousin up with his fifteen-year-old brother.
Episode 100: "Peter and the Wolf"

449 She hurt her back.
Episode 72: "Hawaii Bound"

450 Her diary, which was missing.
Episode 24: "The Possible Dream"

451 Brown.
General

452 Stealing her favorite doll, Kitty KarryAll.
Episode 3: "Kitty KarryAll Is Missing"

453 Bobby finally realized, after having a bad dream, that Jesse James was no hero.

Episode 87: "Bobby's Hero"

454 Carol, whom Marcia had been trying to convince to do a song and dance with her for the Westdale High Family Night Frolics.

Episode 81: "The Show Must Go On"

455 Bobby, who wanted some photography advice from Greg, who was an amateur photographer.

Episode 60: "Click"

456 Greg, who was so sure that he'd become a professional baseball player one day.

Episode 26: "The Dropout"

457 Mike, to whom Carol and Alice were convinced Jan was allergic.

Episode 4: "Katchoo"

458 Greg, who had just finished auditioning for a television talent show with the rest of the kids.

Episode 98: "Adios, Johnny Bravo"

459 Sam.

Episode 97: "The Elopement"

460 His old car.

Episode 53: "The Wheeler Dealer"

461 The family's efforts to save their local park from being torn down in order to build a new county courthouse.

Episode 47: "Double Parked"

462 Marcia, as part of her "Father of the Year" contest essay.

Episode 7: "Father of the Year"

463 Jan, who was desperately trying to find her calling in life.

Episode 106: "Try, Try Again"

464 Bobby, referring to the letter she wrote to Joe Namath so he would come to the house and meet Bobby.

Episode 96: "Mail Order Hero"

465 She had stage fright.

Episode 82: "You Can't Win 'Em All"

466 Cindy.

Episode 67: "Cindy Brady, Lady"

467 The old prospector (Zacchariah T. Brown) the Bradys met in the ghost town they stopped at on their way to the Grand Canyon.
Episode 49: "Ghost Town USA"

468 To return the bad luck idol Bobby found to the tomb of the first king.
Episode 74: "The Tiki Caves"

469 The family began complaining that it was too small.
Episode 18: "To Move or Not to Move"

470 Pay phone.
Episode 9: "Sorry, Right Number"

471 Cindy, who was under the impression that Mike's client was a talent scout looking for a new Shirley Temple.
Episode 113: "The Snooperstar"

472 There had been a mix-up of dates at the theatre where the Brady family was to put on *Snow White and the Seven Dwarfs* in order to raise money to buy Cindy's favorite, retiring teacher a gift.
Episode 95: "Snow White and the Seven Bradys"

473 Alice, who, after walking into a dark house, thought it was a burglar and hit it with her purse.
Episode 77: "Fright Night"

474 Carol, who decided it wouldn't be such a bad idea after she found out Greg had been smoking.
Episode 41: "Where There's Smoke"

475 Alice, who, having just returned from bowling with Sam, walked into a surprise party.
Episode 97: "The Elopement"

476 Peter, to Mike and Carol after they found him in the park feeding pigeons.
Episode 91: "How to Succeed in Business"

477 The kids giving Alice the cold shoulder, which resulted in her packing up and leaving.
Episode 83: "Goodbye, Alice, Hello"

478 Peter.
Episode 64: "Dough Re Mi"

479 To learn more about the little tiki statue Bobby found.
Episode 73: "Pass the Tabu"

480 Alice.
Episode 22: "The Hero"

481 Bobby, who Peter made disappear with his disappearing cabinet trick.
Episode 45: "Lights Out"

482 Greg, who was trying to get Kerry Hathaway, the love of Peter's life, to stop liking him.
Episode 76: "Cyrano De Brady"

483 She was trying to figure out if Jan needed glasses.
Episode 61: "The Not-So-Rose-Colored Glasses"

484 The story of *Alice in Wonderland*, which Cindy asked Carol to read to her while the two were in a used bookstore looking for Marcia's diary (which Cindy mistakenly gave away to a book drive).
Episode 24: "The Possible Dream"

485 Greg, who decided that since he was in high school, he should have his own room.
Episode 43: "Our Son, the Man"

486 Mr. Collins told Bobby how Jesse James had killed his father.
Episode 87: "Bobby's Hero"

487 Sam, referring to tickets for Westdale High's Family Night Frolics.
Episode 81: "The Show Must Go On"

488 Cindy, to Peter, who wanted to know the contents of her latest letter from her secret admirer.
Episode 67: "Cindy Brady, Lady"

489 He worked too slowly.
Episode 91: "How to Succeed in Business"

490 The big, hairy spider that crawled up on him in the middle of the night while in Hawaii.
Episode 73: "Pass the Tabu"

491 Alice.
Episode 24: "The Possible Dream"

492 Her honeymoon.
Pilot: "The Honeymoon"

493 Marcia, after seeing her interviewed on television about her views on Women's Lib.
Episode 44: "The Liberation of Marcia Brady"

494 Alice, after the two argued over whose job was the most difficult.
Episode 8: "The Grass Is Always Greener"

495 Greg, referring to his new part-time job at Mike's firm.
Episode 33: "Call Me Irresponsible"

496 Bobby, who compared basketball to girls.
Episode 99: "Never Too Young"

497 Greg, who felt he needed more space and privacy.
Episode 94: "A Room at the Top"

498 She wanted to change her image so she would
be noticed more.
Episode 42: "Will the Real Jan Brady Please Stand Up?"

499 Alice, after Mike and Carol tried to involve her
in an argument over the great clubhouse debate.
Episode 2: "A Clubhouse Is Not a Home"

500 Peter, talking to Arthur Owens, his double.
Episode 111: "Two Petes in a Pod"

501 Peter, who promised to be Bobby's slave for life.
Episode 105: "My Brother's Keeper"

502 Marcia, who overheard Greg telling Mike what a disaster his idea was
(to introduce Marcia around her first day of high school).
Episode 75: "Today I Am a Freshman"

503 She had been involved in a car accident and was being sued.
Episode 70: "The Fender Benders"

504 Davy Jones.
Episode 63: "Getting Davy Jones"

505 Because his football buddies were giving him a hard time.
Episode 40: "The Drummer Boy"

506 Mike, referring to Beebe Gallini, Mike's cosmetic queen client.
Episode 16: "Mike's Horror-Scope"

507 Vase.
Episode 31: "Confessions, Confessions"

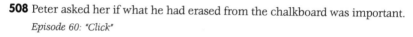

Level Two

508 Peter asked her if what he had erased from the chalkboard was important.
Episode 60: "Click"

509 Peter, who was featured as a hero by the newspaper for saving a little girl's life at a local toy store.
Episode 22: "The Hero"

510 Mike, on the morning of her wedding.
Pilot: "The Honeymoon"

511 Peter.
Episode 76: "Cyrano De Brady"

512 Braces.
Episode 20: "Brace Yourself"

513 Carol's Aunt Jenny.
Episode 66: "Jan's Aunt Jenny"

514 Jan, remembering that the night she lost her locket she had been looking out the window at *The Little Bear*.
Episode 23: "Lost Locket, Found Locket"

515 Slumber party.
Episode 30: "The Slumber Caper"

516 Greg's pet mouse, Myron, who got loose in the house.
Episode 34: "The Impractical Joker"

517 Orange hair.
Episode 116: "The Hair-Brained Scheme"

518 Step.
Episode 14: "Every Boy Does It Once"

519 Bobby, to Greg who was on the phone and couldn't care less.
Episode 65: "The Big Bet"

520 Alice.
Episode 72: "Hawaii Bound"

521 Cindy, although it was only Bobby trying to make Cindy feel older and more desirable.
Episode 67: "Cindy Brady, Lady"

522 "My Hero."
Episode 87: "Bobby's Hero"

523 A wedding invitation to Carol's cousin Gertrude's wedding.
Episode 56: "The Teeter-Totter Caper"

524 Her written driver's test.

Episode 108: "The Driver's Seat"

525 She was a pain to work with.

Episode 52: "Juliet Is the Sun"

526 Joe Namath, who Bobby had pretended to be friends with.

Episode 96: "Mail Order Hero"

527 Tiger's flea powder.

Episode 4: "Katchoo"

528 Kitty KarryAll.

Episode 3: "Kitty KarryAll Is Missing"

529 Marcia, who was scared to death about going to high school.

Episode 75: "Today I Am a Freshman"

530 He was being fired from his job fixing bikes.

Episode 91: "How to Succeed in Business"

531 At Driscoll's Toy Store.

Episode 22: "The Hero"

532 He was trying to write a hit song.

Episode 64: "Dough Re Mi"

533 She was hit by a football.

Episode 90: "The Subject Was Noses"

534 Marcia, who Jan accused of "slinking in" in an effort to steal her boyfriend.

Episode 38: "The Not-So-Ugly Duckling"

535 Marcia's driver's test.

Episode 108: "The Driver's Seat"

536 The "Father of the Year" contest in which Marcia entered Mike.

Episode 7: "Father of the Year"

537 She was an agent looking for a new singer.

Episode 98: "Adios, Johnny Bravo"

538 He was about to get hit by a falling ladder.

Episode 105: "My Brother's Keeper"

539 Moving her bedroom up into the attic.

Episode 94: "A Room at the Top"

540 In the garage.

Episode 24: "The Possible Dream"

541 Den.

Episode 43: "Our Son, The Man"

542 A bike.
Episode 61: "The Not-So-Rose-Colored Glasses"

543 Peter and Greg, because Peter was too afraid to talk to a new girl.
Episode 76: "Cyrano De Brady"

544 Cindy, explaining her sudden fear of the dark.
Episode 45: "Lights Out"

545 Alice, who eventually left the Bradys after the kids began giving her the cold shoulder.
Episode 83: "Goodbye, Alice, Hello"

546 Alice and Sam.
Episode 97: "The Elopement"

547 Cindy, who caught a glimpse of him puffing on a cigarette.
Episode 41: "Where There's Smoke"

548 Cousin Oliver.
Episode 113: "The Snooperstar"

549 The real estate agent who tried to sell the Bradys' house.
Episode 18: "To Move or Not to Move"

550 Cindy, who, along with Bobby, was chosen to take an eligibility test to appear on the *Question the Kids* show.
Episode 82: You Can't Win 'Em All"

551 Don Drysdale.
Episode 26: "The Dropout"

552 Peter's magic act, which he wanted to do in the school's old-time vaudeville show.
Episode 45: "Lights Out"

553 Beebe Gallini, who was upset because Peter's model airplane flew into her hair.
Episode 16: "Mike's Horror-Scope"

554 Sam's meat locker.
Episode 62: "Little Big Man"

555 Bobby and Cousin Oliver, who thought the two men were spies, working against Mike and the FBI.
Episode 115: "Top Secret"

556 UFO.
Episode 110: "Out of This World"

557 To be with his wife and kids.
Episode 19: "Tiger! Tiger!"

558 The kids' Chinese Checkers game.
Episode 21: "The Big Sprain"

559 Phone.
Episode 9: "Sorry, Right Number"

560 It was their contribution to the school carnival.
Episode 57: "My Sister Benedict Arnold"

561 Carol's Aunt Jenny.
Episode 66: "Jan's Aunt Jenny"

562 The first girl Bobby kissed.
Episode 99: "Never Too Young"

563 She passed away.
Pilot: "The Honeymoon"

564 Bobby, who was trying to help Greg fix the shutters while Greg answered a phone call.
Episode 62: "Little Big Man"

565 He had been made a school safety monitor.
Episode 79: "Law and Disorder"

566 The director who asked the Bradys to appear in a laundry detergent commercial.
Episode 59: "And Now a Word from Our Sponsor"

567 Architectural style.
Episode 78: "Career Fever"

568 Jan, whose invitation to Lucy Winter's birthday party was addressed to Marcia by mistake.
Episode 42: "Will the Real Jan Brady Please Stand Up?"

569 Underwear.
Episode 108: "The Driver's Seat"

570 Bobby, who was told to let his new mother take care of a booboo.
Episode 6: "Alice Doesn't Live Here Anymore"

571 Cindy, who was informed that they would be talking about boys at Marcia's slumber party.
Episode 30: "The Slumber Caper"

572 Because Carol and Cindy had to have their tonsils out.
Episode 37: "Coming Out Party"

573 Ice cream.

Episode 104: "Marcia Gets Creamed"

574 A pool table.

Episode 114: "The Hustler"

575 She didn't want them to read the "Dear Libby" column because of the letter she thought one of them had written about the family.

Episode 1: "Dear Libby"

576 The FBI agent who stopped by the house to see Mike.

Episode 115: "Top Secret"

577 Emma.

Episode 69: "Sergeant Emma"

578 Mike's head.

Episode 77: "Fright Night"

579 She lost her voice just before she was supposed to sing in church Christmas morning.

Episode 15: "The Voice of Christmas"

580 A UFO.

Episode 110: "Out of this World"

581 The part of the Fairy Princess in the school play.

Episode 5: "Eenie, Meenie, Mommy, Daddy"

582 Bobby.

Episode 40: "The Drummer Boy"

583 It was Mike's horoscope in one particular episode.

Episode 16: "Mike's Horror-Scope"

584 A guest star to perform at her school prom.

Episode 63: "Getting Davy Jones"

585 At school.

Episode 111: "Two Petes in a Pod"

586 Woodland Park, their local playground, which was going to be torn down to build a new county courthouse.

Episode 47: "Double Parked"

587 Alice, who tried to make sense of a scrambled note.

Episode 48: "Alice's September Song"

588 Greg, who knew that Carol wouldn't take it very well.

Episode 60: "Click"

589 Great Grandma Hutchins, who was coming to visit.

Episode 93: "You're Never Too Old"

590 None. We never saw any.
General

591 The head cheerleader competition, of which Greg was chairman of the selection committee.
Episode 86: "Greg's Triangle"

592 Playing football.
Episode 28: "The Treasure of Sierra Avenue"

593 Bobby, who wanted to join Peter's treehouse club.
Episode 36: "What Goes Up . . . "

594 He had business at King's Island Amusement Park.
Episode 102: "The Cincinnati Kids"

595 George Washington.
Episode 85: "Everyone Can't Be George Washington"

596 Greg.
Episode 89: "Greg Gets Grounded"

597 To make money to buy a car.
Episode 33: "Call Me Irresponsible"

598 He felt sorry for him because he couldn't sell any door-to-door.
Episode 116: "The Hair-Brained Scheme"

599 Mike, who didn't think Carol was being fair about closet space.
Episode 2: "A Clubhouse Is Not a Home"

600 Jan, who received a pretty little locket in the mail one day.
Episode 23: "Lost Locket, Found Locket"

601 Cindy.
Episode 27: "The Baby-sitters"

602 Mike.
Episode 32: "The Tattletale"

603 Jan, in whom Marcia had confided.
Episode 58: "The Private Ear"

604 Jan, who decided she wanted to be an only child.
Episode 80: "Jan, the Only Child"

605 They couldn't decide which doctor they should use, the boys' or the girls'.
Episode 10: "Is There a Doctor in the House?"

606 He made a movie.
Episode 29: "The Un-Underground Movie"

607 She had Greg's pet mouse (his science project for the weekend) exterminated.

Episode 34: "The Impractical Joker"

608 A story about her family for *Tomorrow's Woman* magazine.
Episode 39: "Tell It Like It Is"

609 Marcia.
Episode 44: "The Liberation of Marcia Brady"

610 Marcia, who had a date with the quarterback from Fairview High, the rival school.
Episode 103: "Quarterback Sneak"

611 To adopt another son so their newly adopted boy, Matt, wouldn't feel so lonely.
Episode 107: "Kellys' Kids"

612 Her nephew Oliver was moving in with the Bradys for a while.
Episode 112: "Welcome Aboard"

613 In hopes that it would influence his grade.
Episode 68: "The Power of the Press"

614 Student body president.
Episode 13: "Vote for Brady"

615 Because she got braces.
Episode 20: "Brace Yourself"

616 She took up bug collecting.
Episode 25: "Going, Going . . . Steady"

617 Greg, who was convinced he was going to make it as a professional baseball player.
Episode 26: "The Dropout"

618 David.
Episode 72: "Hawaii Bound"

619 To make her feel older and more desirable.
Episode 67: "Cindy Brady, Lady"

620 Bobby, who was caught pretending to be Jesse James during recess.
Episode 87: "Bobby's Hero"

621 Bobby and Cindy.
Episode 56: "The Teeter-Totter Caper"

622 Driver's ed.
Episode 108: "The Driver's Seat"

623 Marcia, Peter, and Jan.
Episode 52: "Juliet Is the Sun"

624 Kitty KarryAll
Episode 3: "Kitty KarryAll Is Missing"

625 Carol, explaining to Mike what happened just before her car accident.
Episode 70: "The Fender Benders"

626 Peter.
Episode 75: "Today I Am a Freshman"

627 Peter, who was fired from Mr. Martinelli's bike shop.
Episode 91: "How to Succeed in Business"

628 Song.
Episode 64: "Dough Re Mi"

629 "Something suddenly came up."
Episode 90: "The Subject Was Noses"

630 Jan, who was trying to figure out why boys didn't like her.
Episode 38: "The Not-So-Ugly Ducking"

631 He locked them in an old jail cell and stole their car.
Episode 49: "Ghost Town USA"

632 Greg, to his brothers and sisters, after being discovered at a television talent contest tryout.
Episode 98: "Adios, Johnny Bravo"

633 Greg, who had a date with Sandra only if he could find a date for her visiting cousin.
Episode 100: "Peter and the Wolf"

634 He was almost killed by a falling ladder.
Episode 105: "My Brother's Keeper"

635 Greg and Marcia, who sat back to back on a trunk in the attic after both Mike and Carol promised each of them they could move their bedroom into the attic.
Episode 94: "A Room at the Top"

636 Mrs. Desi Arnaz Jr.
Episode 24: "The Possible Dream"

637 Mike, who was a little nervous about performing at the Westdale High Family Night Frolics with Greg.
Episode 81: "The Show Must Go On"

638 Mike's den.
Episode 43: "Our Son, the Man"

639 Peter.
Episode 76: "Cyrano De Brady"

640 Alice, trying to explain to Marcia that she didn't mean to get Marcia in trouble for leaving the stereo on all night.
Episode 83: "Goodbye, Alice, Hello"

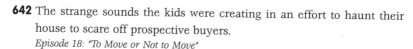

641 Sam, to Alice, who wanted to buy a more traditional wedding gift for Sam's cousin Clara who was engaged.
Episode 97: "The Elopement"

642 The strange sounds the kids were creating in an effort to haunt their house to scare off prospective buyers.
Episode 18: "To Move or Not to Move"

643 To take the qualifying exam for a children's television game show.
Episode 82: "You Can't Win 'Em All"

644 Don Drysdale, who was a client of Mike's.
Episode 26: "The Dropout"

645 Car.
Episode 53: "The Wheeler Dealer"

646 Bobby, who was the only Brady without a trophy.
Episode 46: "The Winner"

647 A camping trip to Mount Claymore.
Episode 12: "A-Camping We Will Go"

648 Mike, while trying to give Greg the old "birds and the bees" talk.
Episode 17: "The Undergraduate"

649 Phones.
Episode 9: Sorry, Right Number"

650 A dunk tank.
Episode 57: "My Sister Benedict Arnold"

651 Jan, who after receiving Aunt Jenny's picture, didn't want to meet her once look-alike.
Episode 66: "Jan's Aunt Jenny"

652 Cindy.
Episode 99: "Never Too Young"

653 It was his wedding day.
Pilot: "The Honeymoon"

654 Greg, who had been fixing a shutter when interrupted by a phone call.
Episode 62: "Little Big Man"

655 Carol's wedding.
Pilot: "The Honeymoon"

656 Bobby, who wasn't too thrilled about being chosen to be a school safety monitor.
Episode 79: "Law and Disorder"

657 In the supermarket parking lot.
Episode 59: "And Now a Word from Our Sponsor"

658 Cindy, after the rest of the Brady kids chose careers for themselves.
Episode 78: "Career Fever"

659 Jan's birthday invitation to Lucy Winter's party.
Episode 42: "Will the Real Jan Brady Please Stand Up?"

660 Jan, who was tired of always hearing about Marcia.
Episode 55: "Her Sister's Shadow"

661 Under a towel.
Episode 88: "The Great Earring Caper"

662 Carol, after Bobby had turned her down to fix his booboo.
Episode 6: "Alice Doesn't Live Here Anymore"

663 As a practical joke on Marcia and her friends at her first slumber party.
Episode 30: "The Slumber Caper"

664 Carol and Cindy, who had to have their tonsils taken out.
Episode 37: "Coming Out Party"

665 Marcia, who got a part-time job at an ice cream parlor.
Episode 104: "Marcia Gets Creamed"

666 Pool table.
Episode 114: "The Hustler"

667 "Dear Libby," the advice columnist.
Episode 1: "Dear Libby"

668 Alice's cousin Emma, who was staying with the Bradys while Alice was on vacation.
Episode 69: "Sergeant Emma"

669 Coaching them for their Safe Soap commercial.
Episode 59: "And Now a Word from Our Sponsor"

670 UFO.
Episode 110: "Out of This World"

671 Cindy, who unbeknownst to her, was allowed to have only one family member come see her in the school play.
Episode 5: "Eenie, Meenie, Mommy, Daddy"

672 The school Glee Club.
Episode 40: "The Drummer Boy"

673 Bugs.
Episode 25: "Going, Going . . . Steady"

674 Alice, during the re-enactment of the events leading up to the disappearance of Jan's locker.
Episode 23: "Lost Locket, Found Locket"

675 Hamper.
Episode 34: "The Impractical Joker"

676 Davy Jones, after learning that he was in town.
Episode 63: "Getting Davy Jones"

677 Skip Farnum Enterprises.
Episode 59: "And Now a Word from Our Sponsor"

678 Dr. Gordon.
Episode 84: "Love and the Older Man"

679 Jan, explaining to Carol why she dropped out of her ballet class.
Episode 106: "Try, Try Again"

680 The family putting on the play *Snow White and the Seven Dwarfs* in order to raise money to buy a special gift for Cindy's retiring teacher, Mrs. Whitfield.
Episode 95: "Snow White and the Seven Bradys"

681 Park.
Episode 47: "Double Parked"

682 Alice's old high school flame who came to town to try and steal her money.
Episode 48: "Alice's September Song"

683 Greg, after she panicked when she saw a huge bruise on his arm, which she assumed was from football practice.
Episode 60: "Click"

684 Great Grandma Hutchins.
Episode 93: "You're Never Too Old"

685 Sam.
General

686 Golf.
Episode 86: "Greg's Triangle"

687 Greg and Peter.
Episode 28: "The Treasure of Sierra Avenue"

688 Voting him into his treehouse club.
Episode 36: "What Goes Up . . . "

689 King's Island Amusement Park.
Episode 102: "The Cincinnati Kids"

690 Bobby, who was trying to convince Mike that Greg's near miss wasn't because he was driving too fast.
Episode 89: "Greg Gets Grounded"

691 He lost then when they slipped out of the cylinder as he stopped to look at hot rod magazines.
Episode 33: "Call Me Irresponsible"

692 Cousin Oliver.
Episode 116: The Hair-Brained Scheme"

693 An egg.
Episode 108: "The Driver's Seat"

694 A locket.
Episode 23: "Lost Locket, Found Locket"

695 He was teaching him what to do when a stranger knocked at the door.
Episode 27: "The Baby-sitters"

696 Alice, who had won the Ever Pressed Fabric Company jingle contest.
Episode 32: "The Tattletale"

697 Peter, who had been bugging the other kids' rooms with Mike's tape recorder.
Episode 58: "The Private Ear"

698 Marcia's first driver's test.
Episode 108: "The Driver's Seat"

699 Jan, who later decided she wanted to be an only child.
Episode 80: "Jan, the Only Child"

700 Because the kids came down with the measles.
Episode 10: "Is There a Doctor in the House?"

701 Greg, who was making a movie for a history class project.
Episode 29: "The Un-Underground Movie"

702 Jan, who was up to her practical jokes again.
Episode 34: "The Impractical Joker"

703 Peter, to help Greg get even with Marcia for trying to join his Frontier Scouts.

Episode 44: "The Liberation of Marcia Brady"

704 Carol.

Episode 103: "Quarterback Sneak"

705 Adopting another son.

Episode 107: "Kellys' Kids"

706 Oliver.

Episode 112: "Welcome Aboard"

707 The drawer full of Checker trading stamps Alice had been saving over the years.

Episode 11: "54-40 and Fight"

708 Bobby, who was beginning to think his family didn't love him.

Episode 14: "Every Boy Does It Once"

709 Carol's favorite vase.

Episode 31: "Confessions, Confessions"

710 Peter.

Episode 35: "A Fistful of Reasons"

711 Scoop Brady.

Episode 68: "The Power of the Press"

712 Marcia, who was competing against her brother for student body president.

Episode 13: "Vote for Brady"

713 Marcia, who had just gotten braces.

Episode 20: "Brace Yourself"

714 Marcia, while in the throes of a mad crush.

Episode 25: "Going, Going . . . Steady"

715 Carol's father, Henry Tyler.

Pilot: "The Honeymoon"

716 Marcia.

Episode 8: "The Grass Is Always Greener"

717 Bobby, as he lay in bed with a mouthful of toothpaste while re-enacting the events that led up to the disappearance of Jan's locket.

Episode 23: "Lost Locket, Found Locket"

718 Buddy.

Episode 35: "A Fistful of Reasons"

719 Voice.

Episode 15: "The Voice of Christmas"

720 Bobby, who was convinced his family no longer loved him.

Episode 14: "Every Boy Does It Once"

721 Math.

Episode 17: "The Undergraduate"

722 Don Ho and his partner.

Episode 72: "Hawaii Bound"

723 Bobby, undercover as Cindy's secret admirer.

Episode 67: "Cindy Brady, Lady"

724 Guards.

Episode 52: "Juliet Is the Sun"

725 Mike.

Episode 4: "Katchoo"

726 Bobby, giving Mike and Carol his alibi when Cindy's favorite doll disappeared.

Episode 3: "Kitty KarryAll Is Missing"

727 She got in a car accident.

Episode 70: "The Fender Benders"

728 Peter, explaining how his homemade volcano worked.

Episode 75: "Today I Am a Freshman"

729 Peter's saving her daughter's life.

Episode 22: "The Hero"

730 Doug Simpson, as he broke his date with her because she had a swollen nose.

Episode 90: "The Subject Was Noses"

731 Jan, who the family felt could use some cheering up.

Episode 38: "The Not-So-Ugly Duckling"

732 They got lost.

Episode 50: "Grand Canyon or Bust"

733 Profile.

Episode 98: "Adios, Johnny Bravo"

734 He was covered in green house paint after pushing Peter out of the way of a falling ladder.

Episode 105: "My Brother's Keeper"

735 She was upset because Mike and Carol decided Greg should have the attic for his room instead of her.
Episode 94: "A Room at the Top"

736 Cindy, who had given the man from the book drive Marcia's diary by mistake.
Episode 24: "The Possible Dream"

737 Mike, referring to what had been his den after Greg moved in.
Episode 43: "Our Son, the Man"

738 He dropped them in the mud.
Episode 76: "Cyrano De Brady"

739 They were mad at her because they thought she had been squealing on them.
Episode 83: Goodbye, Alice, Hello"

740 Alice, who was angry with Sam for telling her she had no class.
Episode 97: "The Elopement"

741 Cindy.
Episode 113: "The Snooperstar"

742 Picked to take the qualifying exam for the *Question the Kids* television game show.
Episode 82: "You Can't Win 'Em All"

743 In the backyard playing catch with Peter.
Episode 26: "The Dropout"

744 Peter, who came home from a party all bummed out because a friend told him he was dull.
Episode 54: "The Personality Kid"

745 Trophy.
Episode 46: "The Winner"

746 In preparation to help the boys with baseball practice after she and Mike decided to switch roles for the day.
Episode 8: "The Grass Is Always Greener"

747 The girls scared them all away with their screaming.
Episode 12: "A-Camping We Will Go"

748 Jan, who thought Carol was going to have a baby when Alice asked her what she thought of the name Linda for a girl.
Episode 17: "The Undergraduate"

749 Cindy, referring to her contribution to the reward for their lost dog, Tiger.
Episode 19: "Tiger! Tiger!"

750 Alice's spraining her ankle while Carol was visiting her sick aunt Mary.
Episode 21: "The Big Sprain"

751 Phone.
Episode 9: "Sorry, Right Number"

752 The bull's eye of the dunk tank the Bradys made for the school carnival.
Episode 57: "My Sister Benedict Arnold"

753 Her great Aunt Jenny.
Episode 66: "Jan's Aunt Jenny"

754 Bobby's first kiss.
Episode 99: "Never Too Young"

755 It was his wedding day.
Pilot: "The Honeymoon"

756 Because she was tired of being in her sister's shadow and it was something Marcia had never done before.
Episode 55: "Her Sister's Shadow"

757 Bobby, who almost fell off the side of the house.
Episode 62: "Little Big Man"

758 His being made a school safety monitor.
Episode 79: "Law and Disorder"

759 The engraving on the silver platter she and the rest of the kids bought for Mike and Carol's anniversary.
Episode 92: "Amateur Nite"

760 Skip Farnum, a TV director who wanted them to be in a soap commercial.
Episode 59: "And Now a Word from Our Sponsor"

761 Bobby, after the rest of the kids chose careers for themselves.
Episode 78: "Career Fever"

762 She wanted to wear them to a costume party.
Episode 88: "The Great Earring Caper"

763 Carol, after she realized that everyone was going to *her* for help instead of their new mom and wife.
Episode 6: "Alice Doesn't Live Here Anymore"

764 The dusty old sleeping bags.
Episode 30: "The Slumber Caper"

765 Marcia, who then hired Peter, then Jan.
Episode 104: "Marcia Gets Creamed"

766 She and Mike decided to go skiing after they weren't able to get reservations at the beach.
Episode 109: "Miss Popularity"

767 A pool table.
Episode 114: "The Hustler"

768 The letter to "Dear Libby," the advice columnist, which Carol was wondering if Mike wrote.
Episode 1: "Dear Libby"

769 Sam, who both Oliver and Bobby thought was a double agent working against Mike and the FBI.
Episode 115: "Top Secret"

770 Alice's cousin Emma.
Episode 69: "Sergeant Emma"

771 The rival high school's stealing Westdale's bear cub mascot.
Episode 101: "Getting Greg's Goat"

772 It got smashed to pieces when Alice walked into a dark house and thought it was an intruder.
Episode 77: "Fright Night"

773 Cindy, rehearsing her part as the Fairy Princess for her school play.
Episode 5: "Eenie, Meenie, Mommy, Daddy"

774 Bobby, who was bummed out because he didn't make the school Glee Club.
Episode 40: "The Drummer Boy"

775 The Davy Jones, Fillmore Junior High Chapter, Fan Club.
Episode 63: "Getting Davy Jones"

776 Peter, who also had a date with another girl that same night.
Episode 111: "Two Petes in a Pod"

777 The kids were all picking names from a hat to see which dwarf they were going to play in *Snow White and the Seven Dwarfs*.
Episode 95: "Snow White and the Seven Bradys"

778 The park closing down so the City could put up a new courthouse.
Episode 47: "Double Parked"

779 Alice's old high school flame, Mark Millard.
Episode 48: "Alice's September Song"

780 Marcia and Jan.
Episode 93: "You're Never Too Old"

Part III

781 Two.
General

782 Surfing.
Episode 86: "Greg's Triangle"

783 The lost wallet Bobby found while playing football with Greg and Peter.
Episode 28: "The Treasure of Sierra Avenue"

784 The girl at the football toss stand, Marge, at King's Island Amusement Park.
Episode 102: "The Cincinnati Kids"

785 Peter and Bobby.
Episode 89: "Greg Gets Grounded"

786 Another chance to work for him after he was fired.
Episode 33: "Call Me Irresponsible"

787 From the boys' clubhouse, which, shortly thereafter, collapsed.
Episode 2: "A Clubhouse Is Not a Home"

788 To find out who sent Jan the mysterious locket in the mail.
Episode 23: "Lost Locket, Found Locket"

789 Cindy, who had a serious tattling problem.
Episode 32: "The Tattletale"

790 Bugging the other kids' rooms with Mike's tape recorder.
Episode 58: "The Private Ear"

791 Egg.
Episode 108: "The Driver's Seat"

792 She was talking about how much easier her friend Donna's life was because she had more privacy than Jan.
Episode 80: "Jan, the Only Child"

793 Because the kids had all come down with the measles.
Episode 10: "Is There a Doctor in the House?"

794 Greg, who was making a movie about the pilgrims for a history class project.
Episode 29: "The Un-Underground Movie"

795 Jan, referring to a phony spider she put in the cookies.
Episode 34: "The Impractical Joker"

796 Carol, who was writing an article about the family for *Tomorrow's Woman* magazine.
Episode 39: "Tell It Like It Is"

797 Marcia's speaking out about Women's Lib on the local news.
Episode 44: "The Liberation of Marcia Brady"

798 Carol's old high school sweetheart.
Episode 103: "Quarterback Sneak"

799 A friend and neighbor of the Bradys who adopted three boys with his wife in one episode.
Episode 107: "Kellys' Kids"

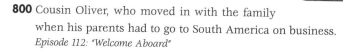

800 Cousin Oliver, who moved in with the family when his parents had to go to South America on business.
Episode 112: "Welcome Aboard"

801 Checker trading stamps.
Episode 11: "54-40 and Fight"

802 Bobby, who felt like the family no longer loved him.
Episode 14: "Every Boy Does It Once"

803 Peter, who let the rest of the kids cover up for him so he wouldn't get grounded from his weekend camping trip.
Episode 31: "Confessions, Confessions"

804 Buddy gave him a black eye.
Episode 35: "A Fistful of Reasons"

805 Rusty wanted to spread a nasty rumor about Marcia, Greg's opponent in the election for student body president.
Episode 13: "Vote for Brady"

806 Nose.
Episode 90: "The Subject Was Noses"

807 Architect.
Episode 78: "Career Fever"

808 He sat on it and crushed it.
Episode 72: "Hawaii Bound"

809 His Kennedy half dollar.
Episode 67: "Cindy Brady, Lady"

810 Bobby and Cindy setting a world's teeter-totter record.
Episode 56: "The Teeter-Totter Caper"

811 Jan, who he thought was allergic to Tiger.
Episode 4: "Katchoo"

Part III

812 Cindy's favorite doll, which was missing.
Episode 3: "Kitty KarryAll Is Missing"

813 Peter's saving a little girl's life.
Episode 22: "The Hero"

814 Reserving a recording studio to record the song he wrote.
Episode 64: "Dough Re Mi"

815 Mike's first boss.
General

816 Zacchariah T. Brown, the old-timer they met while camping in a deserted ghost town on their way to the Grand Canyon.
Episode 49: "Ghost Town USA"

817 She was in his den, secretly writing her essay for the "Father of the Year" contest.
Episode 7: "Father of the Year"

818 The agent who discovered Greg while he and the other kids were trying out for a television talent contest.
Episode 98: "Adios, Johnny Bravo"

819 Her cousin Linda who was coming to town the same weekend she and Greg had a date.
Episode 100: "Peter and the Wolf"

820 Mike and Carol's decision to let Greg have the attic for his bedroom.
Episode 94: "A Room at the Top"

821 There was a man collecting books for a book drive and she thought he had forgotten one.
Episode 24: "The Possible Dream"

822 Voice.
Episode 81: "The Show Must Go On"

823 Greg, who wanted to be more hip.
Episode 43: "Our Son, the Man"

824 Alice, when she decided to leave the Bradys after the kids started giving her the cold shoulder.
Episode 83: "Goodbye, Alice, Hello"

825 Alice, while in a fit of rage.
Episode 97: "The Elopement"

826 A pack of cigarettes fell out of his pocket as he picked up his jacket.
Episode 41: "Where There's Smoke"

827 Marcia, to Jan, who wanted to teach Cindy a good lesson for snooping.
Episode 113: "The Snooperstar"

828 They changed their minds and thought they'd haunt it to scare off prospective buyers.
Episode 18: "To Move or Not to Move"

829 Bobby's certainty that he would pass the qualifying exam both he and Cindy had to take to get on the *Question the Kids* television game show.
Episode 82: "You Can't Win 'Em All"

830 He had business with Mike, who was designing his new house.
Episode 26: "The Dropout"

831 Peter, who was afraid everyone thought he was dull.
Episode 54: "The Personality Kid"

832 Bobby, who was desperately trying to win a trophy.
Episode 46: "The Winner"

833 Alice's.
Episode 12: "A-Camping We Will Go"

834 Greg.
Episode 17: "The Undergraduate"

835 She thought he'd been lured away by burglars so they could take a crack at the Brady house.
Episode 19: "Tiger! Tiger!"

836 Phone bill.
Episode 9: "Sorry, Right Number"

837 Jan.
Episode 109: "Miss Popularity"

838 Her Great Aunt Jenny, who used to look just like Jan as a child.
Episode 66: "Jan's Aunt Jenny"

839 The doctors thought she might have the mumps.
Episode 99: "Never Too Young"

840 His wedding day.
Pilot: "The Honeymoon"

841 Greg, who was looking for a way to make some money to buy a surf board.
Episode 62: "Little Big Man"

842 Bobby, who was made a school safety monitor.
Episode 79: "Law and Disorder"

843 Skip Farnum, a TV director who would later approach the family about making a television commercial for him.
Episode 59: "And Now a Word from Our Sponsor"

844 Anthony and Cleopatra.
Episode 88: "The Great Earring Caper"

845 She felt that she was no longer needed once Carol came into the picture.
Episode 6: "Alice Doesn't Live Here Anymore"

846 The title, "Mrs. Denton: A Hippopotamus," which was written underneath an unflattering picture she had drawn of George Washington while sitting in her English class.
Episode 30: "The Slumber Caper"

847 Marcia, who fired him from Haskell's Ice Cream Hut where she was the afternoon manager.
Episode 104: "Marcia Gets Creamed"

848 Fortune cookies.
Episode 109: "Miss Popularity"

849 The game of pool.
Episode 114: "The Hustler"

850 "Dear Libby."
Episode 1: "Dear Libby"

851 Alice's cousin Emma, an army drill sergeant, was staying with the family while Alice was on vacation.
Episode 69: "Sergeant Emma"

852 Because they tried to scare the girls by creating a "ghost" in the trees and noises in the attic.
Episode 77: "Fright Night"

853 Cindy, who only wanted Santa to bring Carol's voice back.
Episode 15: "The Voice of Christmas"

854 So he and Bobby could take pictures of the UFO they thought they saw out back.
Episode 110: "Out of This World"

855 Bobby, who was down about not making the school Glee Club.
Episode 40: "The Drummer Boy"

856 A pink factory in the shape of a powderpuff.
Episode 16: "Mike's Horror-Scope"

857 Davy Jones.
Episode 63: "Getting Davy Jones"

858 His double, Arthur Owens.
Episode 111: "Two Petes in a Pod"

859 Dopey.
Episode 95: "Snow White and the Seven Bradys"

860 Wings.
Episode 5: "Eenie, Meenie, Mommy, Daddy"

861 Alice, to Sam, referring to her old high school flame who was in town on business.
Episode 48: "Alice's September Song"

862 He was a retired judge.
Episode 93: "You're Never Too Old"

863 Mr. Matthews.
General

864 She wanted to be picked head cheerleader, and Greg was chairman of the judging committee.
Episode 86: "Greg's Triangle"

865 A lost wallet, which Bobby found.
Episode 28: "The Treasure of Sierra Avenue"

866 Buy concert tickets.
Episode 89: "Greg Gets Grounded"

867 Greg, who was working part-time for Mike.
Episode 33: "Call Me Irresponsible"

868 So Carol could wash their clothes and determine which laundry detergent (Safe or Best) was better.
Episode 59: "And Now a Word from Our Sponsor"

869 The girls' taking over the boys' clubhouse.
Episode 2: "A Clubhouse Is Not a Home"

870 Bobby, when Greg asked him what he was doing in the bathroom while the family was supposed to be re-enacting the events that led up to the disappearance of Jan's locket.
Episode 23: Lost Locket, Found Locket"

871 Greg and Marcia, who were left alone for the first time to baby-sit the rest of the kids while Mike and Carol went out for the evening.
Episode 27: "The Baby-sitters"

872 Alice, who won first prize in the Ever Pressed Fabric Company jingle contest.
Episode 32: "The Tattletale"

873 Mike's tape recorder, which Peter had used earlier to tape the other kids' conversations.
Episode 58: "The Private Ear"

874 Marcia, who helped her opponent beat her out for hostess of Senior Banquet Night.
Episode 71: "My Fair Opponent"

875 Jan's desire to be an only child.
Episode 80: "Jan, the Only Child"

876 They decided to go into practice together.
Episode 10: "Is There a Doctor in the House?"

877 Greg, who made a movie about the pilgrims for a history class project.
Episode 29: "The Un-Underground Movie"

878 The article she wrote about her family for *Tomorrow's Woman* magazine.
Episode 39: "Tell It Like It Is"

879 The rival high school's quarterback who used Marcia to steal Greg's football playbook.
Episode 103: "Quarterback Sneak"

880 The adopted Kelly boys who lived next door.
Episode 107: "Kellys' Kids"

881 Oliver.
Episode 112: "Welcome Aboard"

882 The premium catalog for Checker trading stamps.
Episode 11: "54-40 and Fight"

883 Bobby, who decided to run away because he thought the family no longer loved him.
Episode 14: "Every Boy Does It Once"

884 Peter, who broke Carol's favorite vase and let the other kids take the heat so he wouldn't be grounded from his camping trip.
Episode 31: "Confessions, Confessions"

885 Peter, after punching Buddy in the mouth.
Episode 35: "A Fistful of Reasons"

886 Peter, who was having trouble writing his column for the school paper.
Episode 68: "The Power of the Press"

887 She withdrew and supported her opponent, Greg.
Episode 13: "Vote for Brady"

888 Marcia, to Jan, who wanted to know why Marcia wasn't doing her chores.
Episode 25: "Going, Going . . . Steady"

889 For good luck in his surfing contest.
Episode 72: "Hawaii Bound"

890 Marcia, as she and her new boyfriend studied bugs.
Episode 25: "Going, Going . . . Steady"

891 Alice, who just found out she had won a jingle contest.
Episode 32: "The Tattletale"

892 Her wedding, after all hell broke loose.
Pilot: "The Honeymoon"

893 She was wearing his Little Owl costume without his permission.
Episode 2: "A Clubhouse Is Not a Home"

894 Jan, reading her "Most Popular Girl" acceptance speech.
Episode 109: "Miss Popularity"

895 Harvey Klinger, discussing bugs with Marcia on their first date.
Episode 25: "Going, Going . . . Steady"

896 Jesse James.
Episode 87: "Bobby's Hero"

897 Bobby and Cindy on the teeter-totter.
Episode 56: "The Teeter-Totter Caper"

898 Jan, who came home from school all bummed out.
Episode 108: "The Driver's Seat"

899 Marcia, who let her stardom go to her head.
Episode 52: "Juliet Is the Sun"

900 They thought Jan was allergic to him.
Episode 4: "Katchoo"

901 Bobby, who was accused of kidnapping Cindy's favorite doll.
Episode 3: "Kitty KarryAll Is Missing"

902 Car.
Episode 70: "The Fender Benders"

903 The cylinders containing Mike's important designs for King's Island Amusement Park and Jan's Yogi Bear poster.
Episode 102: "The Cincinnati Kids"

904 The Hero of the Month award.
Episode 22: "The Hero"

905 Greg, who wanted to record a song he wrote.
Episode 64: "Dough Re Mi"

906 Jan, who went to the drug store incognito to buy something to get rid of a "friend's" freckles.
Episode 389: "The Not-So-Ugly Duckling"

907 Marcia, in her "Father of the Year" essay.
Episode 7: "Father of the Year"

908 Greg, referring to the deal he was about to make with the music agent who discovered him while he and the other kids were auditioning for a televised talent show.
Episode 98: "Adios, Johnny Bravo"

909 Cousin.
Episode 100: "Peter and the Wolf"

910 Carol, who Marcia was trying to convince to do a duet at the Westdale High Family Night Frolics.
Episode 81: "The Show Must Go On"

911 Greg, who tried hitting on a *senior* during his freshman year.
Episode 43: "Our Son, the Man"

912 Cindy, who was afraid of the dark.
Episode 45: "Lights Out"

913 Alice, to her friend Kay, after deciding to leave the Bradys after the kids started giving her the cold shoulder.
Episode 83: "Goodbye, Alice, Hello"

914 In the garage, where she rode her bike into the picture.
Episode 61: "The Not-So-Rose-Colored Glasses"

915 Having cigarettes.
Episode 41: "Where There's Smoke"

916 It was a phony entry Marcia put in her diary to teach Cindy a lesson for snooping.
Episode 113: "The Snooperstar"

917 Greg, who was trying to tell her to turn down her stereo.
Episode 18: "To Move or Not to Move"

918 Bobby, who built a teepee instead of studying for his eligibility test for the *Question the Kids* television game show.
Episode 82: "You Can't Win 'Em All"

919 Greg.

Episode 26: "The Dropout"

920 Magazines.

Episode 46: "The Winner"

921 In preparation to help Marcia earn her cooking badge after he and Carol switched roles for the day.

Episode 8: "The Grass Is Always Greener"

922 Camping.

Episode 12: "A-Camping We Will Go"

923 Mike, to Greg's math teacher, who requested to see Mike about Greg's poor performance in class.

Episode 17: "The Undergraduate"

924 Tiger, who had been missing for a few days.

Episode 19: "Tiger! Tiger!"

925 Carol was out of town and Alice was laid up in bed with a sprained ankle.

Episode 21: "The Big Sprain"

926 The phone bill, which was astronomical.

Episode 9: "Sorry, Right Number"

927 His first kiss.

Episode 99: "Never Too Young"

928 Carol, the morning of their wedding.

Pilot: "The Honeymoon"

929 Jan.

Episode 55: "Her Sister's Shadow"

930 Bobby, after Sam told him he had a six-inch growth spurt when he was Bobby's age.

Episode 62: "Little Big Man"

931 Bobby, who had gotten his good clothes dirty.

Episode 79: "Law and Disorder"

932 Eighty-five cents a letter.

Episode 92: "Amateur Nite"

933 Skip Farnum, the TV director, who would later approach the family about making a commercial.

Episode 59: "And Now a Word from Our Sponsor"

934 The right drafting materials for designing a house.

Episode 78: "Career Fever"

935 Jan was upset because her party invitation was mistakenly addressed to Marcia.
Episode 42: "Will the Real Jan Brady Please Stand Up?"

936 Marcia.
Episode 88: "The Great Earring Caper"

937 Alice, trying to explain to Mike and Carol why she was leaving the Bradys.
Episode 6: "Alice Doesn't Live Here Anymore"

938 Marcia, explaining how her name got on a paper with a picture and a derogatory remark about her teacher.
Episode 30: "The Slumber Caper"

939 Locket.
Episode 23: "Lost Locket, Found Locket"

940 Bobby.
Episode 32: "The Tattletale"

941 Cindy, after Mike and Carol decided to bring the kids along on their honeymoon.
Pilot: "The Honeymoon"

942 Because Cindy was wearing *his* Indian costume.
Episode 2: "A Clubhouse Is Not a Home"

943 A better time for the family to go out fishing on Mr. Phillips's boat, after Carol and Cindy had their tonsils out.
Episode 37: "Coming Out Party"

944 Helping Jan get elected "Most Popular Girl."
Episode 109: "Miss Popularity"

945 Beating Greg and Peter at pool.
Episode 114: "The Hustler"

946 The signee of the letter written to an advice columnist regarding a similar new family situation to that of the Bradys.
Episode 1: "Dear Libby"

947 Sam, referring to his butcher shop.
Episode 115: "Top Secret"

948 Mike, who was posing for Carol's sculpture.
Episode 77: "Fright Night"

949 Taking pictures of the UFO they spotted while camping out in the backyard.
Episode 110: "Out of This World"

950 She wanted to know how they were going to make her fly when she played the Fairy Princess in the school play.
Episode 5: "Eenie, Meenie, Mommy, Daddy"

951 Peter.
Episode 40: "The Drummer Boy"

952 A re-enactment of the events that led up to the disappearance of Jan's locket.
Episode 23: "Lost Locket, Found Locket"

953 Davy Jones, who she promised to get to sing at her junior high school prom.
Episode 63: "Getting Davy Jones"

954 Peter, to his double, Arthur Owens.
Episode 111: "Two Petes in a Pod"

955 Jan, who was feeling sorry for herself again.
Episode 106: "Try, Try Again"

956 Woodland Park, their local playground, which was about to be torn down to put up a new county courthouse.
Episode 47: "Double Parked"

957 Bobby, who was having trouble taking good photographs.
Episode 60: "Click"

958 Great Grandpa Brady.
Episode 93: "You're Never Too Old"

959 Marcia, Jan, Bobby, and Cindy.
General

960 Driver.
Episode 108: "The Driver's Seat"

961 He fell climbing a tree.
Episode 36: "What Goes Up . . . "

962 Posters from a shop at King's Island Amusement Park.
Episode 102: "The Cincinnati Kids"

963 His classmates were giving him a hard time because he got the part of Benedict Arnold in the school play.
Episode 85: "Everyone Can't Be George Washington"

964 Greg borrowed a friend's car after Mike grounded him from driving for a week.
Episode 89: "Greg Gets Grounded"

965 Greg, who left Mike's important sketches in his car after he gave Greg a lift when his bicycle chain broke.
Episode 33: "Call Me Irresponsible"

966 Hair tonic, which Bobby planned to sell door to door.
Episode 116: "The Hair-Brained Scheme"

967 When she realized her locket was missing.
Episode 23: "Lost Locket, Found Locket"

968 He heard a noise in the backyard, which turned out to be Mike and Carol checking up on them.
Episode 27: "The Baby-sitters"

969 Marcia, to the former class dweeb, who beat out Marcia for hostess for Senior Banquet Night rather unfairly.
Episode 71: "My Fair Opponent"

970 Jan, who told her bothers and sisters she wished she were an only child.
Episode 80: "Jan, the Only Child"

971 The girls' doctor.
Episode 10: "Is There a Doctor in the House?"

972 Myron, a mouse.
Episode 34: "The Impractical Joker"

973 The story she wrote about the Brady family was rejected by a woman's magazine.
Episode 39: "Tell It Like It Is"

974 Peter, who was being coerced by Greg to help him get even with Marcia for trying to join his Frontier Scouts.
Episode 44: "The Liberation of Marcia Brady"

975 So he could get his hands on Greg's football playbook.
Episode 103: "Quarterback Sneak"

976 Ken Kelly, the Bradys' next door neighbor and friend, who just adopted three young boys of various ethnic backgrounds.
Episode 107: "Kellys' Kids"

977 Cousin Oliver.
Episode 112: "Welcome Aboard"

978 Deciding on what premium to purchase with its Checker trading stamps because the company was going out of business.
Episode 11: "54-40 and Fight"

979 Tiger, as Bobby was preparing to run away.
Episode 14: "Every Boy Does It Once"

980 He was grounded for breaking Carol's favorite vase and letting the other kids take the heat for him.
Episode 31: "Confessions, Confessions"

981 Buddy Hinton's dad.
Episode 35: "A Fistful of Reasons"

982 Peter, who was having trouble with his studies after he spent too much time writing his column for the school paper.
Episode 68: "The Power of the Press"

983 Student body president.
Episode 13: "Vote for Brady"

984 He broke his date with her for the school dance, coincidentally, just after she got braces.
Episode 20: "Brace Yourself"

985 Jan, who took Mike's advice to help combat her anxiety during her school debate.
Episode 108: "The Driver's Seat"

986 Chin-ups.
Episode 65: "The Big Bet"

987 Bobby, who idolized Jesse James.
Episode 87: "Bobby's Hero"

988 Teeter-tottering.
Episode 56: "The Teeter-Totter Caper"

989 Jan, who lost her first debate for the Debate Club.
Episode 108: "The Driver's Seat"

990 Playing the part of Juliet's mother in the school play *Romeo and Juliet* after she'd been kicked out of the play for being a pain.
Episode 52: "Juliet Is the Sun"

991 To decide whether or not Bobby kidnapped Cindy's favorite doll, Kitty KarryAll.
Episode 3: "Kitty KarryAll Is Missing"

992 Marcia's fear of starting high school.
Episode 75: "Today I Am a Freshman"

993 He got his first job.
Episode 91: "How to Succeed in Business"

994 Peter, who had just saved a little girl's life.
Episode 22: "The Hero"

995 Greg, who was trying to get the girls to change their minds about start-ing a singing group with him.
Episode 64: "Dough Re Mi"

996 Greg, after Marcia asked him how to break her date with Charley so she could go out with Doug Simpson.
Episode 90: "The Subject Was Noses"

997 Jan, after realizing that it wasn't her freckles that turned boys off.
Episode 38: "The Not-So-Ugly Duckling"

998 Marcia, who had just been caught climbing back in her bedroom win-dow after mailing her "Father of the Year" entry.
Episode 7: "Father of the Year"

999 Greg, referring to the Johnny Bravo suit they were trying to fit on someone.
Episode 98: "Adios, Johnny Bravo"

1000 Peter, referring to the blind date he set Peter up with.
Episode 100: "Peter and the Wolf"

1001 The attic.
Episode 94: "A Room at the Top"

1002 Marcia, referring to her diary, which was now at a used bookstore.
Episode 24: "The Possible Dream"

1003 Alice, to Carol, who was trying to pick out a song for her duet with Marcia at the Westdale High Family Night Frolics.
Episode 81: "The Show Must Go On"

1004 His freshman year, at which time he thought he was too old to be shar-ing a room with kids Peter and Bobby's ages.
Episode 43: "Our Son, the Man"

1005 The portrait of the kids Mike was having taken for Carol's anniversary gift.
Episode 61: "The Not-So-Rose-Colored Glasses"

1006 Cindy, referring to his magic act.
Episode 45: "Lights Out"

1007 Cleopatra.
Episode 20: "Brace Yourself"

1008 The Little Bear.
Episode 23: "Lost Locket, Found Locket"

1009 Natalie Schafer (a.k.a. Lovey Howell).
Episode 113: "The Snooperstar"

1010 Haskell.
Episode 104: "Marcia Gets Creamed"

1011 The portrait Mike had taken of the kids for her anniversary gift.
Episode 61: "The Not-So-Rose-Colored Glasses"

1012 Cage.
Episode 34: "The Impractical Joker"

1013 Bobby accidentally poured hair tonic on them.
Episode 116: "The Hair-Brained Scheme"

1014 Greg, referring to his band.
Episode 41: "Where There's Smoke"

1015 Imogene Coca.
Episode 66: "Jan's Aunt Jenny"

1016 Greg, referring to the mouse he brought home from school for his science project.
Episode 34: "The Impractical Joker"

1017 Oahu.
Episode 72: "Hawaii Bound"

1018 Three days.
Episode 91: "How to Succeed in Business"

1019 Mt. Claymore.
Episode 43: "Our Son, the Man"

1020 Checker trading stamps.
Episode 11: "54-40 and Fight"

1021 4222 Clinton Way.
Episode 23: "Lost Locket, Found Locket"

1022 Cindy, who questioned the entire family because she thought they were all talking about her behind her back.
Episode 113: "The Snooperstar"

1023 So she could go out with Doug Simpson.

Episode 90: "The Subject Was Noses"

1024 To get back at Marcia for inviting Warren Mulaney to the house.

Episode 57: "My Sister Benedict Arnold"

1025 Marcia, referring to getting someone to perform at her school prom.

Episode 63: "Getting Davy Jones"

1026 Greg, who was trying to write a song.

Episode 64: "Dough Re Mi"

1027 Eleven.

Episode 65: "The Big Bet"

1028 Don Drysdale, to Mike, who was designing a new home for him.

Episode 26: "The Dropout"

1029 A safari outfit.

Episode 59: "And Now a Word from Our Sponsor"

1030 It was the message inside the fortune cookies Alice made for Jan's "Most Popular Girl" election.

Episode 109: "Miss Popularity"

1031 Driscoll's Toy Store.

Episode 22: "The Hero"

1032 Pork chops and applesauce.

Episode 54: "The Personality Kid"

1033 Peter, who wanted to do a magic act.

Episode 45: "Lights Out"

1034 Up on a ladder in the back of the house.

Episode 62: "Little Big Man"

1035 Building a house of cards.

Episode 115: "Top Secret"

1036 Harry.

General

1037 At the Golden Spoon Diner, where she took a job after leaving the Bradys.

Episode 83: "Goodbye, Alice, Hello"

1038 Silver Platters.

Episode 92: "Amateur Nite"

1039 Tommy Jamison.

Episode 67: "Cindy Brady, Lady"

1040 Harvey Klinger's.
Episode 25: "Going, Going Steady"

1041 Tent.
Episode 12: "A-Camping We Will Go"

1042 Cindy, who was told along with the rest of the kids to remember to pitch in and get the housework done while Alice was laid up in bed with a sprained ankle.
Episode 21: "The Big Sprain"

1043 Greg's new room, which had previously been Mike's den.
Episode 43: "Our Son, the Man"

1044 Bobby, who had just been named school safety monitor.
Episode 79: "Law and Disorder"

1045 The Coolidge High mascot Greg hid in his room after his football team stole it.
Episode 101: "Getting Greg's Goat"

1046 Molly Webber.
Episode 71: "My Fair Opponent"

1047 Mike.
Episode 10: "Is There a Doctor in the House?"

1048 Greg, referring to Marcia being interviewed about her views on Women's Lib.
Episode 44: "The Liberation of Marcia Brady"

1049 "The Whole Truth."
Episode 68: "The Power of the Press"

1050 To ask her to the school dance in an effort to boost her self-confidence after getting braces.
Episode 20: "Brace Yourself"

1051 "Hark!"
Episode 52: "Juliet Is the Sun"

1052 "What America Means to Me."
Episode 55: "Her Sister's Shadow"

1053 Jan, who wished she was an only child.
Episode 80: "Jan, the Only Child"

1054 Jan and Cindy.
Episode 77: "Fright Night"

1055 Eleven hundred dollars.
Episode 28: "The Treasure of Sierra Avenue"

1056 Matthew Kelly, their newly adopted son.
Episode 107: "Kellys' Kids"

1057 Bobby, to his friends, lying about being good friends with Joe Namath.
Episode 96: "Mail Order Hero"

1058 To mail her "Father of the Year" entry.
Episode 7: "Father of the Year"

1059 Participating in the Westdale High Family Night Frolics.
Episode 81: "The Show Must Go On"

1060 Alice, who had no idea that the Brady family was under the mistaken impression that Alice was going to elope with Sam on their usual bowling night.
Episode 97: "The Elopement"

1061 Burt Grossman.
Episode 18: "To Move or Not to Move"

1062 Greg, referring to his first car.
Episode 53: "The Wheeler Dealer"

1063 She found a love letter he had written to her in his coat pocket.
Episode 17: "The Undergraduate"

1064 Carol, to Mike, on their wedding day.
Pilot: "The Honeymoon"

1065 Bobby and Cindy, who were in the midst of Fire Safety Awareness Week at school.
Episode 54: "The Personality Kid"

1066 Alice came along and put the dirty towels in the laundry bag, along with the earrings.
Episode 88: "The Great Earring Caper"

1067 Her cousin Emma, who stayed with the Bradys while Alice was on vacation.
Episode 69: "Sergeant Emma"

1068 Bobby, who didn't realize he would get Greg into trouble.
Episode 89: "Greg Gets Grounded"

1069 Priscilla.
Episode 29: "The Un-Underground Movie"

1070 The dent in the station wagon from Carol's accident.
Episode 70: "The Fender Benders"

1071 Jan, who had a major crush on Clark.
Episode 38: "The Not-So-Ugly Duckling"

1072 Cindy, which then made Bobby the only Brady without a trophy.
Episode 46: "The Winner"

1073 The bike Jan mistakenly took home from the school playground.
Episode 61: "The Not-So-Rose-Colored Glasses"

1074 Greg and Peter, who were discussing Peter's bad luck streak in the job hunting area.
Episode 104: "Marcia Gets Creamed"

1075 Martin.
Pilot: "The Honeymoon"

1076 Jan, referring to her nonstop sneezing.
Episode 4: "Katchoo"

1077 Greg, to Marcia, referring to the purposefully bad architectural design he made so Mike would *have* to tell him he didn't have the talent to be an architect.
Episode 78: "Career Fever"

1078 It was the note Cindy left Alice, referring to Mark Millard, an old high school flame, who called to say he was in town.
Episode 48: "Alice's September Song"

1079 Gertrude.
Episode 56: "The Teeter-Totter Caper"

1080 Dr. Vogel had asked Mike if Marcia was free on Friday night.
Episode 84: "Love and the Older Man"

1081 Peter, Jan, and Cindy.
Episode 40: "The Drummer Boy"

1082 Greg making the school football team, which they knew Carol would be unhappy about.
Episode 60: "Click"

1083 Her Great Grandma Hutchins.
Episode 93: "You're Never Too Old"

1084 Jennifer Nichols.
Episode 86: "Greg's Triangle"

1085 No.
Episode 99: "Never Too Young"

1086 The only thing Cindy wanted for Christmas was Carol's voice to come back in time to sing in church on Christmas morning.
Episode 15: "The Voice of Christmas"

1087 Her new dentist, Dr. Vogel.
Episode 84: "Love and the Older Man"

1088 Woodland Park.
Episode 47: "Double Parked"

1089 Bobby, who saved Peter's life.
Episode 105: "My Brother's Keeper"

1090 Peter.
Episode 36: "What Goes Up . . . "

1091 *Hal Barton's TV Talent Review.*
Episode 98: "Adios, Johnny Bravo"

1092 Cindy, who passed the test but couldn't answer a single question on the show because she had stage fright.
Episode 82: "You Can't Win 'Em All"

1093 A broken down barnacle barge.
Episode 37: "Coming Out Party"

1094 Marcia's new boyfriend, Jerry Rogers, a football rival of Greg's.
Episode 103: "Quarterback Sneak"

1095 Desi Arnaz Jr.
Episode 24: "The Possible Dream"

1096 At the beginning of the fourth season.
General

1097 Frontier Scouts.
Episode 44: "The Liberation of Marcia Brady"

1098 George Washington.
Episode 30: "The Slumber Caper"

1099 She found out she had won the Ever Pressed Fabric Company jingle contest.
Episode 32: "The Tattletale"

1100 The girls' cat before they moved in with Mike and the boys.
Pilot: "The Honeymoon"

1101 Mumps.
Episode 99: "Never Too Young"

1102 Student body president.
Episode 13: "Vote for Brady"

1103 Toothpaste.
Episode 23: "Lost Locket, Found Locket"

1104 Lincoln.
General

1105 The head cheerleader competition.
Episode 86: "Greg's Triangle"

1106 Suckers.
Episode 10: "Is There a Doctor in the House?"

1107 Puppy love.
Episode 17: "The Undergraduate"

1108 Wig.
Episode 42: "Will the Real Jan Brady Please Stand Up?"

1109 Santa.
Episode 15: "The Voice of Christmas"

1110 Marcia, who pretended to be sick on her first day of high school.
Episode 75: "Today I Am a Freshman"

1111 Brigadier General James McDivitt.
Episode 110: "Out of This World"

1112 Jan, referring to the picture of her once-look-alike aunt Jenny.
Episode 66: "Jan's Aunt Jenny"

1113 Jan, who pulled one too many practical jokes when she took and lost Greg's mouse.
Episode 34: "The Impractical Joker"

1114 The little tiki statue he found while in Hawaii.
Episode 72: "Hawaii Bound"

1115 When the kids tried to decide what premium to buy with their trading stamps.
Episode 11: "54-40 and Fight"

1116 Cindy, who was looking for her favorite doll.
Episode 3: "Kitty KarryAll Is Missing"

1117 Alice, who left the Bradys for a short period of time.
Episode 83: "Goodbye, Alice, Hello"

1118 His car.
Episode 53: "The Wheeler Dealer"

1119 Cindy snooping in Marcia's diary.
Episode 113: "The Snooperstar"

1120 The Indian boy who befriended a lost Bobby and Cindy at the bottom of the Grand Canyon.
Episode 51: "The Brady Braves"

1121 The disappearing cabinet trick.
Episode 45: "Lights Out"

1122 Her date with Charley.
Episode 90: "The Subject Was Noses"

1123 Cindy, who hung by the boys' belts on the clothes line to practice flying for her part as the Fairy Princess in the school play.
Episode 5: "Eenie, Meenie, Mommy, Daddy"

1124 They had all heard the rumor that Marcia was going to get Davy Jones to sing at their prom.
Episode 63: "Getting Davy Jones"

1125 Peter, to Greg, who was planning to record his song solo before Peter gave him the idea to get the Brady kids together and form a group.
Episode 64: "Dough Re Mi"

1126 Mike's old high school sweetheart.
Episode 65: "The Big Bet"

1127 The fourth season.
General

1128 He was a pitcher.
Episode 26: "The Dropout"

1129 "Boy Hero."
Episode 22: "The Hero"

1130 So Mike and the kids could sneak out and have a portrait taken for Carol's anniversary gift.
Episode 61: "The Not-So-Rose-Colored Glasses"

1131 Cindy, who let her upcoming appearance on the *Question the Kids* television game show go to her head.
Episode 82: "You Can't Win 'Em All"

1132 Peter, whose voice was changing as the kids rehearsed for their recording session.
Episode 64: "Dough Re Mi"

1133 A swing set.
Episode 62: "Little Big Man"

1134 A silver convertible, two brown station wagons, two blue convertibles, and a red convertible.
General

1135 Cindy's two male rabbits.
Episode 116: "The Hair-Brained Scheme"

1136 Alice's.

Episode 34: "The Impractical Joker"

1137 Jan, who picked it up (as well as picking up a big, hairy spider).
Episode 72: "Hawaii Bound"

1138 Mr. Martinelli.

Episode 91: "How to Succeed in Business"

1139 Bobby's paper on Jesse James being his hero.
Episode 87: "Bobby's Hero"

1140 She was suggesting it be Greg's new bedroom.
Episode 43: "Our Son, the Man"

1141 Debate.

Episode 108: "The Driver's Seat"

1142 The Checker trading stamps they were fighting over.
Episode 11: "54-40 and Fight"

1143 Holding a mock trial to decide Bobby's fate.
Episode 3: "Kitty KarryAll Is Missing"

1144 Alice's announcement that she would be leaving the Bradys.
Episode 83: "Goodbye, Alice, Hello"

1145 The Little Bear.

Episode 23: "Lost Locket, Found Locket"

1146 They wanted to see if she would read Marcia's diary.
Episode 113: "The Snooperstar"

1147 A love-struck Peter.

Episode 76: "Cyrano De Brady"

1148 Davy Jones.

Episode 63: "Getting Davy Jones"

1149 A baton.

Episode 106: "Try, Try Again"

1150 In the supermarket parking lot where Skip Farnum, a TV director, was following the family around.
Episode 59: "And Now a Word from Our Sponsor"

1151 Rachel, Greg's date at the drive-in.
Episode 65: "The Big Bet"

1152 Mike was going to sneak the kids out to have a portrait taken for Carol's anniversary gift.
Episode 61: "The Not-So-Rose-Colored Glasses"

1153 Greg, to Jan, who had promised Herman that Greg would help him in order to get his vote for "Most Popular Girl."
Episode 109: "Miss Popularity"

1154 Pink.
Episode 16: "Mike's Horror-Scope"

1155 Greg (Mike's office, Sam's butcher shop), Marcia (Haskell's Ice Cream Hut), Peter (Mr. Martinelli's Bike Shop, Haskell's Ice Cream Hut, The Leaning Tower of Pizza) and Jan (Haskell's Ice Cream Hut).
General

1156 Sam sarcastically told her to let the postman take her out the night Cindy told him Alice couldn't come to the phone because she was hugging the postman.
Episode 32: "The Tattletale"

1157 Bobby and Cindy's attempt to set a new teeter-tottering record.
Episode 56: "The Teeter-Totter Caper"

1158 At a neighbor's house a couple of blocks away with his "wife and kids."
Episode 19: "Tiger! Tiger!"

1159 Bobby, who was upset with Cindy for wearing his Indian costume.
Episode 2: "A Clubhouse Is Not a Home"

1160 Her secret admirer, which was Bobby, disguising his voice on the phone.
Episode 67: "Cindy Brady, Lady"

1161 Setting Peter up by giving him Mike's tape recorder with a prerecorded conversation, after the two older kids thought he wasn't punished enough for bugging the kids' rooms.
Episode 58: "The Private Ear"

1162 Peter knocked his tooth loose.
Episode 35: "A Fistful of Reasons"

1163 Marcia, after Carol told her she could go steady with Harvey Klinger.
Episode 25: "Going, Going . . . Steady"

1164 They used a bear puppet to create a shadow on their tent.
Episode 12: "A-Camping We Will Go"

1165 Sam decided to take someone else to the Meat Cutter's Ball after Alice slipped on the Chinese Checkers game board and sprained her ankle.
Episode 21: "The Big Sprain"

1166 "Dear Libby."
Episode 1: "Dear Libby"

1167 After seeing *Cinderella*, Bobby felt like a neglected stepchild.
Episode 14: "Every Boy Does It Once"

1168 Peter, who was given the responsibility of punishing his brothers and sisters after each of them confessed to breaking Carol's favorite vase to cover up for Peter.
Episode 31: "Confessions, Confessions"

1169 Jill.
Episode 79: "Law and Disorder"

1170 His rival high school's mascot, which he and his football buddies kidnapped.
Episode 101: "Getting Greg's Goat"

1171 He was too old.
Episode 44: "The Liberation of Marcia Brady"

1172 Alice, who was giving Peter some advice on how to write his column for the school paper.
Episode 68: "The Power of the Press"

1173 His parents were taking him out of town that same weekend.
Episode 20: "Brace Yourself"

1174 The part of Juliet in the school play *Romeo and Juliet*.
Episode 52: "Juliet Is the Sun"

1175 The girl who *really* won first place in the essay contest on Americanism, after Jan was told *she* won.
Episode 55: "Her Sister's Shadow"

1176 Arthur Owens, his double.
Episode 111: "Two Petes In a Pod"

1177 Peter, who tried everything to get out of playing Benedict Arnold in the school play.
Episode 85: "Everyone Can't Be George Washington"

1178 The girl Greg was dating while he worked part-time for Mike.
Episode 33: "Call Me Irresponsible"

1179 The charity hoedown the Bradys were planning to attend when Jan suddenly decided she wanted to be an only child.
Episode 80: "Jan, the Only Child"

1180 The kids needed $56.23 to pay for the engraving on the silver platter they bought for Mike and Carol's anniversary.
Episode 92: "Amateur Nite"

1181 Paula Tardy, who wrote an unflattering remark about their English teacher below Marcia's drawing.

Episode 30: "The Slumber Caper"

1182 Marcia, who along with her sisters tried to scare the boys out of the attic.

Episode 77: "Fright Night"

1183 A response to the Bradys' ad in the Lost and Found for the wallet the boys found.

Episode 28: "The Treasure of Sierra Avenue"

1184 He was Asian.

Episode 107: "Kelly's Kids"

1185 Joe Namath, who came to visit Bobby after Cindy wrote him, claiming to be a very, very sick Bobby.

Episode 96: "Mail Order Hero"

1186 That she had entered Mike in the "Father of the Year" contest.

Episode 7: "Father of the Year'

1187 Poem.

Episode 81: "The Show Must Go On"

1188 She saw Bobby and Cindy run through the house dressed up as ghosts so no one would buy the Brady house.

Episode 18: "To Move or Not to Move"

1189 Greg's friend Eddie, who was trying to sell Greg his old car.

Episode 53: "The Wheeler Dealer"

1190 Miss Linda O'Hara.

Episode 17: "The Undergraduate"

1191 Tommy Johnson, who cleared Greg's name.

Episode 41: "Where There's Smoke"

1192 The pool table Mr. Matthews gave Mike in appreciation for a job well done.

Episode 114: "The Hustler"

1193 Alice's cousin Emma, to Mike and Carol.

Episode 69: "Sergeant Emma"

1194 The frog Bobby entered in a frog-jumping contest.

Episode 89: "Greg Gets Grounded"

1195 Movie.

Episode 29: "The Un-Underground Movie"

1196 The guy who took Carol to court after *he* hit the Bradys' station wagon in the supermarket parking lot.
Episode 70: "The Fender Benders"

1197 She and Bobby spied Jan rubbing lemon on her face.
Episode 38: "The Not-So-Ugly Duckling"

1198 Subscriptions.
Episode 46: "The Winner"

1199 The driving contest between her and Greg.
Episode 108: "The Driver's Seat"

1200 Peter, to Marcia, after she fired him from his job at Haskell's Ice Cream Hut because he was lazy.
Episode 104: "Marcia Gets Creamed"

1201 Marcia, referring to her and Greg running for student council.
Episode 13: "Vote for Brady"

1202 Jan and Cindy.
Episode 41: "Where There's Smoke"

1203 Getting rid of Tiger when they thought Jan was allergic to him.
Episode 4: "Katchoo"

1204 The phone bill.
Episode 9: "Sorry, Right Number"

1205 Peter, to Mike and Carol, who was convinced he was dying of a fatal illness after reading a medical book.
Episode 78: "Career Fever"

1206 Mark Millard, Alice's old high school flame.
Episode 48: "Alice's September Song"

1207 Carol's knitting.
Episode 112: "Welcome Aboard"

1208 A silver frog.
Episode 56: "The Teeter-Totter Caper"

1209 The Calderons.
Episode 100: "Peter and the Wolf"

1210 Marcia being upset over Mike and Carol's decision to let Greg have the attic.
Episode 94: "A Room at the Top"

1211 His football teammates, who were giving him a hard time for being in the school Glee Club.
Episode 40: "The Drummer Boy"

1212 Practicing for a Roaring Twenties bash.
Episode 99: "Never Too Young"

1213 "Oh Come All Ye Faithful."
Episode 15: "The Voice of Christmas"

1214 Marcia's gorgeous new dentist, Dr. Vogel.
Episode 84: "Love and the Older Man"

1215 Park.
Episode 47: "Double Parked"

1216 Peter, who had devoted himself to being his younger brother's slave for life after Bobby saved *his* life.
Episode 105: "My Brother's Keeper"

1217 Bobby, who was laid up in bed after spraining his ankle.
Episode 36: "What Goes Up . . . "

1218 He told them Jesse James had carved his initials on the wall.
Episode 49: "Ghost Town USA"

1219 Greg, referring to the music agent whom the kids met while auditioning for a televised talent show.
Episode 98: "Adios, Johnny Bravo"

1220 Bobby, referring to the eligibility test for the *Question the Kids* television game show.
Episode 82: "You Can't Win 'Em All"

1221 That she had tonsillitis.
Episode 37: "Coming Out Party"

1222 A Yogi Bear poster.
Episode 102: "The Cincinnati Kids"

1223 Jan's tap dancing.
Episode 106: "Try, Try Again"

1224 Jerry Rogers, who was trying to get his hands on Greg's football playbook by using Marcia.
Episode 103: "Quarterback Sneak"

1225 The kids were picking names from a hat to see which dwarf they got to play in the Bradys' production of *Snow White and the Seven Dwarfs*.
Episode 95: "Snow White and the Seven Bradys"

1226 Marcia, to Greg's friends, on her first day of high school.
Episode 75: "Today I Am a Freshman"

1227 Greg, to Marcia, explaining how he made his phony UFO.
Episode 110: "Out of This World"

1228 Bobby, to Cindy and Oliver, who were trying to start their own business after their first attempts at selling hair tonic and breeding rabbits failed.
Episode 116: "The Hair-Brained Scheme"

1229 To take Greg's mouse as a joke.
Episode 34: "The Impractical Joker"

1230 Waikiki.
Episode 72: "Hawaii Bound"

1231 Martinelli.
Episode 91: "How to Succeed in Business"

1232 C+.
Episode 87: "Bobby's Hero"

1233 Drivers.
Episode 108: "The Driver's Seat"

1234 The kids working together to pick out a gift the whole family would enjoy from the Checker trading stamp premium catalog.
Episode 11: "54-40 and Fight"

1235 The kids were shunning Bobby after Cindy accused him of stealing her favorite doll.
Episode 3: "Kitty KarryAll Is Missing"

1236 Alice, lying to Carol about having to leave the Bradys to manage her Uncle Winston's dress shop.
Episode 83: "Goodbye, Alice, Hello"

1237 Mr. Gunther.
Episode 95: "Snow White and the Seven Bradys"

1238 Wallpaper samples.
Episode 90: "The Subject Was Noses"

1239 Movie studio.
Episode 112: "Welcome Aboard"

1240 Peter, referring to the man at the recording studio where Greg wanted to record his song.
Episode 64: "Dough Re Mi"

1241 Expanding his butcher shop.
Episode 115: "Top Secret"

1242 Five (1969–1974).
General

1243 Sunflower Girls.
Episode 44: "The Liberation of Marcia Brady"

1244 Skateboard.
Episode 32: "The Tattletale"

1245 She was commenting on how nervous he was on his wedding day.
Pilot: "The Honeymoon"

1246 Frontier Scout.
Episode 44: "The Liberation of Marcia Brady"

1247 Truth or Dare, and a laughing game called HA.
Episode 30: "The Slumber Caper"

1248 The campaign poster she was making for Marcia's student body president election.
Episode 13: "Vote for Brady"

1249 Designs.
Episode 33: "Call Me Irresponsible"

1250 Winston.
Episode 83: "Goodbye, Alice, Hello"

1251 Harvey.
Episode 25: "Going, Going . . . Steady"

1252 Kirby's Pet Shop.
Episode 116: "Hair-Brained Scheme"

1253 The Banana Convention.
Episode 41: "Where There's Smoke"

1254 Carol's Aunt Jenny, referring to Jan, who was convinced she was going to look like her great aunt when she got older.
Episode 66: "Jan's Aunt Jenny"

1255 Jan, who shoved Greg's mouse in the girls' faces.
Episode 34: "The Impractical Joker"

1256 Old Mr. Hanalei.
Episode 73: "Pass the Tabu"

1257 Jesse James, whose life Mike wanted Bobby to read about.
Episode 87: "Bobby's Hero"

1258 That men were better drivers than women.
Episode 108: "The Driver's Seat"

1259 Checker trading stamps.
Episode 11: "54-40 and Fight"

1260 Alice, to Marcia, who accused Alice of snitching on her.
Episode 83: "Goodbye, Alice, Hello"

1261 The typewriter that typed the mailing label on the package sent to Jan dropped its Ys.
Episode 23: "Lost Locket, Found Locket"

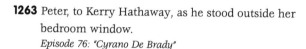

1262 Oliver, to Cindy, who just asked if he wanted to help her find out if there was a secret everyone was hiding from her.
Episode 113: "The Snooperstar"

1263 Peter, to Kerry Hathaway, as he stood outside her bedroom window.
Episode 76: "Cyrano De Brady"

1264 Mike, who was helping Cindy with her rehearsal for the school play.
Episode 5: "Eenie, Meenie, Mommy, Daddy"

1265 Davy Jones, who wrote a letter to Marcia because she was the president of his Fillmore Junior High Fan Club.
Episode 63: "Getting Davy Jones"

1266 Greg, who locked his brothers out of the room while he was trying to write a song.
Episode 64: "Dough Re Mi"

1267 Practicing pitching in the backyard.
Episode 26: "The Dropout"

1268 Kathy Williams.
Episode 109: "Miss Popularity"

1269 Tina Spencer.
Episode 22: "The Hero"

1270 Cindy, who wanted Peter to make Bobby reappear again after vanishing in his disappearing cabinet trick.
Episode 45: "Lights Out"

1271 He was secretly enlarging his butcher shop.
Episode 115: "Top Secret"

1272 Zacchariah T. Brown, the old prospector they met in the ghost town, and Mr. Matthews, Mike's second boss.
General

1273 Doll.
Episode 3: "Kitty KarryAll Is Missing"

1274 Greg, who was laughed at by his brothers and sisters for trying to act cool.
Episode 43: "Our Son, the Man"

1275 Greg, who, along with his brother, set up a burglar trap after overhearing Alice tell Mike and Carol about the latest rash of burglaries in their neighborhood.
Episode 19: "Tiger! Tiger!"

1276 Cindy was wearing his Indian costume without his permission.
Episode 2: "A Clubhouse Is Not a Home"

1277 Marcia, after she thought Jan had told Peter something Marcia had told her in confidence.
Episode 58: "The Private Ear"

1278 Learning how to fight.
Episode 35: "A Fistful of Reasons"

1279 Air mattress.
Episode 12: "A-Camping We Will Go"

1280 She asked him how he was going to support himself once he ran away.
Episode 14: "Every Boy Does It Once"

1281 At the dinner table.
Episode 31: "Confessions, Confessions"

1282 Bobby, who was unhappy about being appointed school safety monitor.
Episode 79: "Law and Disorder"

1283 Coolidge High.
Episode 101: "Getting Greg's Goat"

1284 Dr. Cameron.
Episode 10: "Is There a Doctor in the House?"

1285 Peter, who joined Marcia's Sunflower Girls to help Greg prove a point.
Episode 44: "The Liberation of Marcia Brady"

1286 Mr. Price.
Episode 68: "The Power of the Press"

1287 "Who goes there?!"
Episode 52: "Juliet Is the Sun"

1288 Essay.
Episode 55: "Her Sister's Shadow"

1289 Marcia's first slumber party.
Episode 30: "The Slumber Caper"

1290 They found a slide projector in their room containing a slide of the "ghost."
Episode 77: "Fright Night"

1291 Twenty dollars.
Episode 28: "The Treasure of Sierra Avenue"

1292 Ken and Kathy Kelly's bigot of a neighbor.
Episode 107: "Kelly's Kids"

1293 Joe Namath, referring to Bobby.
Episode 96: "Mail Order Hero"

1294 Mike, who could see that *nothing* could tear Harvey and Marcia away from their bugs.
Episode 25: "Going, Going . . . Steady"

1295 His and hers bowling balls.
Episode 97: "The Elopement"

1296 Wes Parker.
Episode 17: "The Undergraduate"

1297 Carol, to Mike, who brought the dog to her parents' house on their wedding day.
Pilot: "The Honeymoon"

1298 Jan, who thought she'd help Alice out.
Episode 88: "The Great Earring Caper"

1299 Her cousin Emma, who was filling in for Alice while on vacation.
Episode 69: "Sergeant Emma"

1300 Greg, who was trying to make a film about the pilgrims for a history class project.
Episode 29: "The Un-Underground Movie"

1301 Marcia, who Jan was convinced was flirting with her latest crush.
Episode 38: "The Not-So-Ugly Duckling"

1302 Mike and Carol, who were each brushing up in preparation to switch roles for the day.
Episode 8: "The Grass Is Always Greener"

1303 Greg, to his student body election campaign manager, who wanted to start a rumor about Marcia, Greg's opponent.
Episode 13: "Vote for Brady"

1304 She came down with the mumps.
Episode 52: "Juliet Is the Sun"

1305 Alice, to Mike, referring to Carol, whom the family frequently bypassed for Alice in their time of need.
Episode 6: "Alice Doesn't Live Here Anymore"

1306 Her cousin Gertrude's wedding, to which Bobby and Cindy weren't invited.
Episode 56: "The Teeter-Totter Caper"

1307 Greg's old high school buddy who was in college and looking for a roommate.
Episode 94: "A Room at the Top"

1308 Bobby, who didn't make the school Glee Club.
Episode 40: "The Drummer Boy"

1309 Linette Carter.
Episode 60: "Click"

1310 Carol's grandmother.
Episode 93: "You're Never Too Old"

1311 Marcia, referring to the head cheerleader competition of which Greg was chairman of the judging committee.
Episode 86: "Greg's Triangle"

1312 In the backyard.
Episode 99: "Never Too Young"

1313 Jan, to Marcia, who had a crush on her new dentist.
Episode 84: "Love and the Older Man"

1314 He wanted to find out why the city was going to tear down the local park to put up a building.
Episode 47: "Double Parked"

1315 Bobby's claim that Marcia's new boyfriend tried to steal Greg's football playbook.
Episode 103: "Quarterback Sneak"

1316 They had been following an Indian boy.
Episode 49: "Grand Canyon or Bust"

1317 Bobby and Cindy, who wound up eating everything in sight at King's Island amusement park.
Episode 102: "The Cincinnati Kids"

1318 She couldn't cut it as a ballerina.
Episode 106: "Try, Try Again"

1319 Jerry Rogers, Westdale High's rival quarterback.
Episode 103: "Quarterback Sneak"

1320 Alice's unexpected departure from the Brady house.
Episode 83: "Goodbye, Alice, Hello"

1321 A Yogi Bear poster.
Episode 102: "The Cincinnati Kids"

1322 Sam, who was exaggerating about his experience in the army to impress Bobby and Oliver.
Episode 115: "Top Secret"

1323 Cousin Oliver, who asked Carol how bunny rabbits were made.
Episode 116: "The Hair-Brained Scheme"

1324 Her secretary, Hazel.
Episode 66: "Jan's Aunt Jenny"

1325 In the garage.
Episode 34: "The Impractical Joker"

1326 Greg, who wiped out in a surfing competition in Hawaii.
Episode 72: "Hawaii Bound"

1327 Checker trading stamps.
Episode 11: "54-40 and Fight"

1328 They did a re-enactment of the events leading up to its disappearance.
Episode 23: "Lost Locket, Found Locket"

1329 Cindy, who was convinced there was something going on that had to do with her.
Episode 113: "The Snooperstar"

1330 Kerry Hathaway, Jan's pretty, new friend.
Episode 76: "Cyrano De Brady"

1331 Doug Simpson.
Episode 90: "The Subject Was Noses"

1332 Mike, who was helping Cindy rehearse for her school play.
Episode 5: "Eenie, Meenie, Mommy, Daddy"

1333 Davy Jones, who was in town, but unreachable.
Episode 63: "Getting Davy Jones"

1334 One hundred and fifty nonreturnable dollars.
Episode 64: "Dough Re Mi"

1335 Nineteen.
Episode 65: "The Big Bet"

1336 Don Drysdale.
Episode 26: "The Dropout"

1337 Margie Whipple, who was infatuated with Peter, was going to be there.
Episode 42: "Will the Real Jan Brady Please Stand Up?"

1338 Peter's picture was on the front page of the newspaper after he saved a little girl's life.
Episode 22: "The Hero"

1339 Sam, who didn't realize how sensitive Bobby was about his height.
Episode 62: "Little Big Man"

1340 Harvest Gold.
General

1341 Marcia, who had just passed the Frontier Scout's initiation.
Episode 44: "The Liberation of Marcia Brady"

1342 Leaving Alice's new stereo on.
Episode 32: "The Tattletale"

1343 Doll, kazoo.
Episode 3: "Kitty KarryAll Is Missing"

1344 Greg, who thought he was too old to call his parents "Mom" and "Dad."
Episode 43: "Our Son, the Man"

1345 Peter, who sat in the park feeding pigeons all day after being fired from his first job.
Episode 91: "How to Succeed in Business"

1346 Helping Sam hang curtains at his apartment.
Episode 27: "The Baby-sitters"

1347 Bugging the kids' rooms with Mike's tape recorder.
Episode 58: "The Private Ear"

1348 An editor for *Tomorrow's Woman* magazine.
Episode 39: "Tell It Like It Is"

1349 Ralph.
Episode 35: "A Fistful of Reasons"

1350 Beebe Gallini, to Mike.
Episode 16: "Mike's Horror-Scope"

1351 Marcia, to Harvey Klinger, after she realized that going steady creates too much pressure.
Episode 25: "Going, Going . . . Steady"

1352 The advice columnist, also known as "Dear Libby."
Episode 1: "Dear Libby"

1353 Senior Banquet Night, where Marcia was one of the co-hostesses.
Episode 71: "My Fair Opponent"

1354 Primate.
Episode 68: "The Power of the Press"

1355 Mike, Carol, and Alice.
Episode 20: "Brace Yourself"

1356 Marcia, who was kicked out of the play *Romeo and Juliet* because she was a pain to work with.
Episode 52: "Juliet Is the Sun"

1357 Pamela Phillips, referring to Peter's double.
Episode 111: "Two Petes in a Pod"

1358 Randi Petersen and her father.
Episode 33: "Call Me Irresponsible"

1359 Patty's Prancing Poodles.
Episode 92: "Amateur Night"

1360 Itching powder in the sleeping bags, a glowing skull in the refrigerator, or a bucket over the door.
Episode 30: "The Slumber Caper"

1361 The sculpture Carol made of Mike after it had been smashed and put back together again.
Episode 77: "Fright Night"

1362 Mr. Stoner, the old man who lost the wallet Bobby found while playing football.
Episode 28: "The Treasure of Sierra Avenue"

1363 The Kelly family, who Alice found sitting in the Bradys' family room in the middle of the night.
Episode 107: "Kelly's Kids"

1364 The family ski trip.
Episode 7: "Father of the Year"

1365 Yes. In the episode where the family thought Alice and Sam eloped, Alice announced that the two were engaged.
Episode 97: "The Elopement"

1366 Cindy, referring to her two male rabbits.
Episode 116: "The Hair-Brained Scheme"

1367 Aristotle Onassis's.
Episode 66: "Jan's Aunt Jenny"

1368 In the doghouse.
Episode 34: "The Impractical Joker"

1369 Bobby's popcorn.
Episode 72: "Pass the Tabu"

1370 Marcia.
Episode 108: "The Driver's Seat"

1371 Ninety-four.
Episode 11: "54-40 and Fight"

1372 She found her lost locket.
Episode 23: "Lost Locket, Found Locket"

1373 Penelope Fletcher.
Episode 113: "The Snooperstar"

1374 Kerry Hathaway, after Greg pretended to be a "love-'em-and-leave-'em" kind of guy in an effort to scare her off.
Episode 76: "Cyrano De Brady"

1375 Big man on campus.
Episode 90: "The Subject Was Noses"

1376 The special performance the children gave of the school play so that Cindy could invite her entire family.
Episode 5: "Eenie, Meenie, Mommy, Daddy"

1377 Davy Jones.
Episode 63: "Getting Davy Jones"

1378 "When It's Time to Change."
Episode 64: "Dough Re Mi"

1379 With an umbrella.
Episode 65: "The Big Bet"

1380 Two thousand boxes of Safe laundry detergent.
Episode 59: "And Now a Word from Our Sponsor"

1381 Peter, who was dateless for the "Most Popular Girl and Boy" dance.
Episode 109: "Miss Popularity"

1382 A Dracula costume.
Episode 111: "Two Petes in a Pod"

1383 Bobby, who had just climbed out of the meat locker window at Sam's butcher shop where he and Greg were locked in.
Episode 62: "Little Big Man"

1384 Nelson.
General

1385 Alice, who saw two little ghosts run past her bedroom.
Episode 18: "To Move or Not to Move"

1386 $50.
Episode 53: "The Wheeler Dealer"

1387 The top of the salt shaker, after Mike poured the whole shaker of salt on his eggs.
Episode 32: "The Tattletale"

1388 Greg, to his new agent, just before he ripped his contract and walked out.
Episode 98: "Adios, Johnny Bravo

1389 Harry.
Episode 114: "The Hustler"

1390 Frog.
Episode 89: "Greg Gets Grounded"

1391 Skip Farnum, the director of the Safe soap commercial.
Episode 59: "And Now a Word from Our Sponsor"

1392 The witness stand, where Cindy would have to testify that she didn't see Carol look back before she backed out of her parking place.
Episode 70: "The Fender Benders"

1393 Jan's imaginary boyfriend.
Episode 38: "The Not-So-Ugly Duckling"

1394 He found out that Mike and Carol told all their friends to buy subscriptions from him.
Episode 46: "The Winner"

1395 The Leaning Tower of Pizza.
Episode 104: "Marcia Gets Creamed"

1396 Campaign.
Episode 13: "Vote for Brady"

1397 Carol had been talking on Mike's phone to her friend Martha when Martha got upset and ran off crying without hanging up the receiver.
Episode 9: "Sorry, Right Number"

1398 Warren had beat out Greg for first string on the basketball team.
Episode 57: "My Sister Benedict Arnold"

1399 Mark Millard, Alice's old high school flame who came to town to swindle her out of all her money.
Episode 48: "Alice's September Song"

1400 He got nailed by pies.
Episode 112: "Welcome Aboard"

1401 Peter, after being caught playing Don Juan at the same restaurant where Mike and Carol were entertaining a client and his wife.
Episode 100: "Peter and the Wolf"

1402 They tried to wear her out by calling her downstairs to the phone every few minutes.
Episode 94: "A Room at the Top"

1403 UFO.
Episode 110: "Out of This World"

1404 Her secret family recipe, which Peter had erased from the blackboard after days of trying to remember it.
Episode 60: "Click"

1405 Pat Conway.
Episode 86: "Greg's Triangle"

1406 Mike encouraging the family's all-out campaign to save Woodland Park, the site where Mike's firm was going to build a new county courthouse.
Episode 47: "Double Parked"

1407 Clip the hedges and polish his shoes.
Episode 105: "My Brother's Keeper"

1408 The Brady's plan to help Bobby get over his fear of heights with a trampoline.
Episode 36: "What Goes Up . . . "

1409 He didn't think his grandfather, Chief Dan Eagle Cloud, understood his desire to become an astronaut.
Episode 51: "The Brady Braves"

1410 Greg, who ripped up his newly signed music contract with his agents before walking out.
Episode 98: "Adios, Johnny Bravo"

1411 Boat.
Episode 37: "Coming Out Party"

1412 Jan, referring to Mike's important sketches she lost at King's Island after accidentally switching cylinders with Mike.
Episode 102: "The Cincinnati Kids"

1413 The girls' ballet teacher.
Episode 106: "Try, Try Again"

1414 The coach found out he stole Greg's phony playbook.
Episode 103: "Quarterback Sneak"

1415 The audience waiting in the backyard, who came to see the Bradys' production of *Snow White and the Seven Dwarfs.*
Episode 95: "Snow White and the Seven Bradys"

1416 Captain McCartney, who was sent to the Brady house to investigate the alleged UFO sighting.
Episode 110: "Out of This World"

1417 Job.
Episode 83: "Goodbye, Alice, Hello"

1418 Locking Sam and his landlord in the meat locker.
Episode 115: "Top Secret"

1419 Her wedding day.
Pilot: "The Honeymoon"

1420 Carol's Aunt Jenny.
Episode 66: "Jan's Aunt Jenny"

1421 Gwynevere.
Episode 34: "The Impractical Joker"

1422 Vincent Price.
Episode 74: "The Tiki Caves"

1423 His nightmare about Jesse James killing his family.
Episode 87: "Bobby's Hero"

1424 How close Marcia got to the egg.
Episode 108: "The Driver's Seat"

1425 A sewing machine.
Episode 11: "54-40 and Fight"

1426 Shirley Temple.
Episode 113: "The Snooperstar"

1427 Peter, who couldn't get his lines right as he stood outside Kerry Hathaway's bedroom window.
Episode 76: "Cyrano De Brady"

1428 Nose.
Episode 90: "The Subject Was Noses"

1429 Cindy, who could only invite one parent to see her in the school play.
Episode 5: "Eenie, Meenie, Mommy, Daddy"

1430 Davy Jones after Marcia kissed him on the cheek.
Episode 63: "Getting Davy Jones"

1431 Recording studio.
Episode 64: "Dough Re Mi"

1432 Baseball.
Episode 26: "The Dropout"

1433 The actress friend of the Bradys who helped Mike and Carol learn their lines for the Safe soap commercial.
Episode 59: "And Now a Word from Our Sponsor"

1434 Jan, who lost a lot of friends after being elected "Most Popular Girl" at school.
Episode 109: "Miss Popularity"

1435 Peter, who finally realized how big his head had gotten after saving a little girl's life.
Episode 22: "The Hero"

1436 The portrait of the kids Mike had taken for Carol's anniversary gift, which Jan rode her bike into.
Episode 54: "The Not-So-Rose-Colored Glasses"

1437 Bobby, who was about to try crawling out of the small meat locker door window where he and Greg were locked in.
Episode 62: "Little Big Man"

1438 Marcia.
General

1439 Bobby, to Greg, referring to the convertible top.
Episode 65: "The Big Bet"

1440 Mrs. Huntsicker.
Episode 18: "To Move or Not to Move"

1441 Cosmetic.
Episode 16: "Mike's Horror-Scope"

1442 She rejected it.
Episode 3: "Kitty KarryAll Is Missing"

1443 Mike's den, which Greg turned into a bedroom.
Episode 43: "Our Son, the Man"

1444 The clubhouse Mike and the boys were going to build for the girls.
Episode 2: "A Clubhouse Is Not a Home"

1445 Harvey.
Episode 25: "Going, Going . . . Steady"

1446 Cindy, after the kids thought one of the parents was unhappy with the new marriage.
Episode 1: "Dear Libby"

1447 Carol insulting Mike's boss when she thought it was Mike on the phone disguising his voice.
Episode 37: "Coming Out Party"

1448 "Don't play ball in the house."
Episode 31: "Confessions, Confessions"

1449 Mascot stealing.
Episode 101: "Getting Greg's Goat"

1450 Marcia, who was trying to help Peter pass his science test.
Episode 68: "The Power of the Press"

1451 The three boys who came over to the house to ask Marcia to the school dance were all asked to come over by Mike, Carol, and Alice, to help Marcia feel better after getting braces.
Episode 20: "Brace Yourself"

1452 Ninety-four.
Episode 55: "Her Sister's Shadow"

1453 Mike's boss's niece, whom he thought he'd set up with Peter.
Episode 111: "Two Petes In a Pod"

1454 Practicing potato sack racing for the charity hoedown they were all going to.
Episode 80: "Jan, the Only Child"

1455 *The Pete Sterne Amateur Hour.*
Episode 92: "Amateur Nite"

1456 Diary.
Episode 113: "The Snooperstar"

1457 An infatuated classmate of Jan's.
Episode 23: "Lost Locket, Found Locket"

1458 Alice, who the kids were planning to scare that night when she returned from her date with Sam.
Episode 77: "Fright Night"

1459 In the living room upon returning home from work.
Episode 7: "Father of the Year"

1460 Sam, who Alice was trying to make jealous after the two had a fight.
Episode 81: "The Show Must Go On"

1461 The Meat Packers.
Episode 97: "The Elopement"

1462 It fell out of his pocket while he was changing a flat tire.
Episode 28: "The Treasure of Sierra Avenue"

1463 Greg, who had just bought a lemon.
Episode 53: "The Wheeler Dealer"

1464 Wallpaper.
Episode 90: "The Subject Was Noses"

1465 Mike, referring to the "Linda" Greg had a crush on.
Episode 17: "The Undergraduate"

1466 Jan, who wanted Peter to announce the New Jan Brady at a friend's party.
Episode 42: "Will the Real Jan Brady Please Stand Up?"

1467 Two hundred and fifty-six.
Episode 114: "The Hustler"

1468 Jan, who was going to wear her new wig.
Episode 42: "Will the Real Jan Brady Please Stand Up?"

1469 The Bradys' backyard.
Episode 107: "Kelly's Kids"

1470 Studying for a test in bed.
Episode 23: "Lost Locket, Found Locket"

1471 Peter's flattering article about his extremely tough science teacher in the school paper.
Episode 68: "The Power of the Press"

1472 "On the Good Ship Lollipop."
Episode 113: "The Snooperstar"

1473 Beebe Gallini.
Episode 16: "Mike's Horror-Scope"

1474 *The Three Musketeers.*
Episode 107: "Kelly's Kids"

1475 He threw his briefcase on the floor.
Episode 70: "The Fender Benders"

1476 Jan.
Episode 38: "The Not-So-Ugly Duckling"

1477 She still had time to get Davy Jones to sing at her prom.
Episode 63: "Getting Davy Jones"

1478 *Cartoon King.*
> Episode 46: "The Winner"

1479 The Brady kids came in third in the televised amateur contest they entered.
> Episode 92: "Amateur Nite"

1480 At the local TV station where Davy Jones had been interviewed the day before.
> Episode 63: "Getting Davy Jones"

1481 Because he was out with another girl.
> Episode 104: "Marcia Gets Creamed"

1482 That she was seen in the balcony of the movie theatre with Felix Brown.
> Episode 13: "Vote for Brady"

1483 Mike, after everyone tried to scrub Jan's allergy to Tiger right off him.
> Episode 4: "Katchoo"

1484 Because Kathy beat out Marcia for the cheerleading squad, he invited her over to the house to practice cheers.
> Episode 57: "My Sister Benedict Arnold"

1485 Greg, who purposefully drew bad sketches so Mike would have to tell him he would never make it as an architect.
> Episode 78: "Career Fever"

1486 *Gypsy.*
> Episode 81: "The Show Must Go On"

1487 Peter, who was trying to speed up the process of his voice changing.
> Episode 64: "Dough Re Mi"

1488 She was rehearsing for a play.
> Episode 33: "Call Me Irresponsible"

1489 Monty Marshall.
> Episode 82: "You Can't Win 'Em All'"

1490 High school.
> Episode 75: "Today I Am a Freshman"

1491 The salesman at the department store who sold the Brady kids the silver platter they bought for Mike and Carol's anniversary.
> Episode 92: "Amateur Nite"

1492 Twinkles.
> Episode 103: "Quarterback Sneak"

1493 Carter Air Force Base.
> Episode 110: "Out of This World"

1494 Aunt Jenny, whose cast was signed by lots of famous people.

Episode: 66: "Jan's Aunt Jenny"

1495 Mike, who Carol said was away on business.

Episode 116: "The Hair-Brained Scheme"

1496 Ann.

Pilot: "The Honeymoon"

1497 Talking on the phone.

Episode 105: "My Brother's Keeper"

1498 So she wouldn't have to be in the school play and have to choose between her parents, of whom she was only allowed to invite one.

Episode 5: "Eenie, Meenie, Mommy, Daddy"

1499 She had twisted her ankle in gym class.

Episode 45: "Lights Out"

1500 Marathon Studio.

Episode 112: "Welcome Aboard"

Part Four

The Episode Guide

"The Honeymoon"

PILOT:

Written by Sherwood Schwartz
Directed by John Rich
Original Airdate: September 26, 1969

This is where it all began. Mike Brady and Carol Martin, each with three children from previous marriages, come together as one, and from this day forward are forever known as *The Brady Bunch*. In this pilot, we find ourselves in the backyard of Carol's parents' home where she and Mike are about to exchange wedding vows in front of family, friends, and house pets. But we soon realize all *won't* be going smoothly when dog and cat meet. The couple does exchange nuptials, but not without incident.

And if that isn't enough to make us wonder about this family, just wait until the honeymoon. The newlyweds decide to share their wedded bliss with the entire family, and before we know it, the entire Brady bunch is marching up the stairs past the concierge, who looks on, probably the same way the rest of us did, as if the family were nuts. He was right.

"Dear Libby"

EPISODE 1:

Written by Lois Hire
Directed by John Rich
Original Airdate: October 3, 1969

Marcia mistakenly believes a letter written to an advice columnist expressing frustration over the writer's new marriage and three new stepchildren was written by one of her parents. Soon everyone is jumping to conclusions and they all secretly write letters to "Dear Libby," begging to find out who wrote the original letter signed *Harried and Hopeless*. But when Libby pays an unexpected visit to the Brady house, she reassures the family that the original letter came from clear across the country.

"A Clubhouse Is Not a Home"

Written by Skip Webster
Directed by John Rich
Original Airdate: October 31, 1969

EPISODE 2:

The boys are having a hard time adjusting to the fact that there are four more women in their house, so they start hanging out in their "boys' clubhouse" for some good old-fashioned male bonding. The girls don't think it's fair that the boys have their own place, so they pretty much take over the clubhouse after Mike gives the old "share-and-share-alike" lecture. This doesn't exactly fly with the boys, and soon after, all hell breaks loose. When Mike and the boys build the girls their own clubhouse, not realizing Bobby got the nails for the new one from the old one, the boys' clubhouse collapses and now it's the boys' turn to take over the girls' clubhouse.

"Kitty KarryAll Is Missing"

Written by Al Schwartz and Bill Freedman
Directed by John Rich
Original Airdate: November 7, 1969

EPISODE 3:

Cindy accuses Bobby of stealing Kitty KarryAll, her favorite doll, and Bobby accuses Cindy of stealing his favorite kazoo. A mock trial is held, but the jury comes back deadlocked and nothing is resolved. Then, after seeing how distraught she is over her loss, Bobby decides to buy his sister a new Kitty KarryAll, but she rejects it because it's not the real Kitty. In the end, however, we discover who the real culprit is, Tiger.

"Katchoo"

Written by William Cowley
Directed by John Rich
Original Airdate: October 24, 1969

EPISODE 4:

The family thinks Jan is allergic to Tiger and no one knows what to do. After several baths, as well as a lot of tears, Mike and Carol decide to ship him off to Grandma's house. Poor Jan. She feels just awful about it. But when she carries Tiger's new flea powder out to the car just as Mike drives off to Grandma's house, the family discovers it was the new flea powder she was allergic to and not Tiger at all.

"Eenie, Meenie, Mommy, Daddy"

Written by Joanna Lee
Directed by John Rich
Original Airdate: October 10, 1969

EPISODE 5:

Cindy gets the coveted role of the fairy princess in her school play. She's ecstatic until she discovers she is allowed only one ticket and doesn't know who to invite, her old mommy or her new daddy. After a lot of agonizing and tears, she still can't decide, but by now I think we all know that Cindy will get her way. As it turns out, the entire Brady bunch is invited to attend a "special performance" put on especially for the Brady family (like none of the other kids in the play shared the two-parent dilemma).

"Alice Doesn't Live Here Anymore"

Written by Paul West
Directed by John Rich
Original Airdate: October 17, 1969

EPISODE 6:

Alice decides the Brady family doesn't need her anymore now that there is a new full-time mom in the picture, so she uses the old "sick-aunt-in-Seattle" story as an excuse to take off. The problem is, Alice gets her cities-beginning-with-S's mixed up and the family begins to catch on. Naturally, the family isn't about to let her leave (who would fill in the ninth square?), so they all pretend to be totally helpless to prove to her she's indispensable.

"Father of the Year"

Written by Skip Webster
Directed by George Cahan
Original Airdate: January 2, 1970

EPISODE 7:

Marcia enters Mike in a local "Father of the Year" contest, and stays up late each night until she finishes her essay. Even when Mike punishes Marcia after finding her in his den well after her bedtime, she's still determined he win. But late one night after everyone's in bed, Marcia discovers her entry must be postmarked by midnight that night, so she climbs out of her bedroom window and mails it. Carol and Mike discover her missing, and upon her return she's busted big-time! Mike is furious and punishes her when she refuses to explain herself, banning her from the family ski trip. Marcia's devastated but manages to keep a lid on it until Mike is awarded "Father of the Year" and all is forgiven.

"The Grass Is Always Greener"

Written by David P. Harmon
Directed by George Cahan
Original Airdate: March 13, 1970

EPISODE 8:

Mike and Carol decide to settle the age-old dispute over whose job is harder. Carol takes on an afternoon of ball with the boys while Mike helps Marcia earn her cooking badge. Murphy's Law prevails and the ending is predictable. No one wins.

"Sorry, Right Number"

Written by Ruth Brooks Flippen
Directed by George Cahan
Original Airdate: November 21, 1969

EPISODE 9:

The kids' continual bickering over the telephone prompts Mike to install a payphone. Bad idea. When Mike has to use the payphone to make the business deal of a lifetime (because Carol's on his phone discussing hemlines with Martha), the operator cuts in demanding ten cents. And guess who hasn't got any change? Mike eventually calls back to explain, but the guy isn't interested in excuses until Mike explains why he was calling from a payphone. Luckily the guy has teenagers of his own and just loves the idea of the payphone, so he gives Mike a second chance.

"Is There a Doctor in the House?"

Written by Ruth Brooks Flippen
Directed by Oscar Rudolph
Original Airdate: December 26, 1969

EPISODE 10:

All the kids come home from school with the measles so Carol calls the girls' doctor (Marion Ross, a.k.a. Richie Cunningham's mom), and Mike calls the boys' doctor. Mike and Carol seem to think it's a real problem to have two doctors, so much of a problem in fact, that they overlook the obvious solution until the end of the show: keep both doctors.

"54-40 and Fight"

Written by Burt Styler
Directed by Oscar Rudolph
Original Airdate: January 9, 1970

EPISODE 11:

The kids discover they must redeem their Checker trading stamps before the Checker Trading Stamp Company goes out of business. When they can't decide on a premium the whole family can enjoy, they decide to build a house of cards to determine who gets to choose the premium, the boys or the girls. Remember this one? Marcia doesn't even think to remove her clunky charm bracelet even though she almost knocks the whole thing over. But soon enough, Tiger charges in and knocks it down on the boys' turn and the girls win. Bless their hearts, though, instead of getting a sewing machine, they surprise the boys with a color TV.

"A-Camping We Will Go"

Written by Herbert Finn and Alan Dinehart
Directed by Oscar Rudolph
Original Airdate: November 14, 1969

EPISODE 12:

Carol and Mike decide that taking the whole family on a camping trip might help bring them all closer together. The boys don't like the idea of the girls intruding upon their annual camping trip, and the girls have no interest in going along. No matter though, because they've all got to go anyway. And of course, everything that could go wrong does, and no one's really having any fun. But we can't have any unhappy endings in this family, so naturally, everything turns around in the end.

"Vote for Brady"

Written by Elroy Schwartz
Directed by David Alexander
Original Airdate: December 12, 1969

EPISODE 13:

Greg and Marcia run against each other for student council. This turns into a full-blown family rivalry, and there is no peace in the Brady household. Marcia even accuses Alice of wanting Greg to win because she's known him longer. In the end, following Greg's campaign speech, Marcia takes the podium and announces her withdrawal from the election.

"Every Boy Does It Once"

Written by Lois and Arnold Peyser
Directed by Oscar Rudolph
Original Airdate: December 5, 1969

EPISODE 14:

Bobby thinks no one loves him anymore. He lets his imagination run away from him when, after watching *Cinderella* on TV, Carol asks him to sweep the chimney. Then his brothers and stepsisters are suddenly too busy for him. Bobby decides he's not going to take this kind of treatment and packs up his bags, but Greg catches wind of his plans and tells the folks. Using a little reverse-psychology, Mike and Carol manipulate him into staying.

"The Voice of Christmas"

Written by John Fenton Murray
Directed by John Rudolph
Original Airdate: December 19, 1969

Carol comes down with laryngitis on Christmas Eve, and she can't sing at church on Christmas Day. Everyone is crushed, but Cindy comes up with a plan. Why not ask Santa Claus to bring her voice back? Naturally, he promises he will. How could he say no to such a sweet girl? Suddenly, in the middle of the night, Carol wakes up humming "Oh Come, All Ye Faithful" in her sleep, and wouldn't you know, she miraculously gets her voice back.

"Mike's Horror-Scope"

Written by Ruth Brooks Flippen
Directed by Oscar Rudolph
Original Airdate: January 16, 1970

Carol reads Mike's horoscope, which says a mysterious stranger will enter into his life. Next thing we know, Mike's got a new client named Beebe Gallini who wants him to design her new cosmetic factory to look like a fluffy powder puff. After Mike begins spending late nights and weekends at the office catering to Beebe's every whim, Carol begins to worry that she's lost Mike forever. Of course, Mike Brady's too smart to succumb to the wily charms of a pink-feathered diva.

"The Undergraduate"

Written by David P. Harmon
Directed by Oscar Rudolph
Original Airdate: January 23, 1970

Greg has a crush on a mysterious Linda. Carol and Alice can't keep their noses out of his business and start questioning the girls about all the Lindas they know. They even think they've found her when Marcia brings home a new classmate, but then Mike suddenly announces he's found the right Linda—Miss Linda O'Hara, Greg's math teacher. But the love affair doesn't last long once Greg meets her fiancé. No, he doesn't want her anymore, he's more interested in him, Wes Parker of the Los Angeles Dodgers.

"To Move or Not to Move"

Written by Paul West
Directed by Oscar Rudolph
Original Airdate: March 6, 1970

EPISODE 18:

The kids have had it with their close quarters, so Mike and Carol decide it's time to buy a bigger house. But as soon as they find a buyer, the kids realize they don't want to move anymore and decide to haunt the house, hoping to scare away the buyer. The real estate agent thinks it's disgraceful once they find out the kids are behind it, but the buyer thinks it's lovely. The family stays put and they're all suddenly able to adjust to what was once an absolutely unbearable situation.

"Tiger! Tiger!"

Written by Elroy Schwartz
Directed by Herb Wallerstein
Original Airdate: January 30, 1970

EPISODE 19:

Tiger disappears and the boys freak out and put an ad in the newspaper offering a $42.76 reward, but there are no takers. Meanwhile, Alice is convinced he was lured away by burglars who've targeted the Brady house. When the boys overhear her sharing her concerns to Mike and Carol, they set up a booby trap . . . except the only booby they trap is a mud-masked Alice. Soon after, everyone in the Brady family gets on their bike and scouts the neighborhood. Tiger has been doing a little scouting of his own and they find him across town. Apparently, Tiger's got a new "girlfriend" . . . and a couple of adorable puppies to boot.

"Brace Yourself"

Written by Brad Radnitz
Directed by Oscar Rudolph
Original Airdate: February 13, 1970

EPISODE 20:

Marcia gets braces and is convinced they're the reason Alan Anthony has canceled his date with her, even after he explains he has to go out of town with his parents. *Marcia, Marcia, Marcia*, you're so vain! No one can take her incessant whining any longer, so Mike, Carol, and Alice each con three boys into asking her out. But they all show up at the same time and Marcia gives them the boot. Then, at the eleventh hour, Alan's parents change their plans and Alan takes Marcia to the dance after all. And Marcia's dentist must have changed his plans because by the next episode, she's not wearing braces anymore.

"The Big Sprain"

Written by Tam Spiva
Directed by Russ Mayberry
Original Airdate: February 6, 1970

EPISODE 21:

Alice sprains her ankle while Carol is out of town, and the whole family has to pitch in with the household duties. The girls don't know how to make toast and the boys don't know how to wash a dish, and all hell breaks loose. Meanwhile, not only is Alice mending a sprained ankle, but also a broken heart. Seems Sam still plans to go to the Meat Cutter's Ball while Alice is laid up . . . and he isn't going stag. Once again, everything ends up okay. Alice gets her man and the family gets their mom.

"The Hero"

Written by Elroy Schwartz
Directed by Oscar Rudolph
Original Airdate: February 20, 1970

EPISODE 22:

Peter saves a little girl's life at Driscoll's Toy Store (remember the wall that comes crashing down?). Anyway, now Peter's a hero with a big ego and everyone's getting sick of hearing his everchanging tale. He even decides to throw himself a party honoring himself, but no one wants to come. Get over yourself, Peter.

"Lost Locket, Found Locket"

Written by Charles Hoffman
Directed by Norman Abbott
Original Airdate: March 20, 1970

EPISODE 23:

Jan starts moaning about being a middle child. Then, out of the blue, she receives a mysterious locket with no card attached and no one has a clue who sent it . . . except that the typewriter that typed the card drops its Ys. Then one night, Jan discovers her locket is missing. She's absolutely frantic and the whole family joins forces to help her find it. Through a re-enactment of the events that led up to its disappearance, Jan finds it dangling in the trees outside her bedroom window. In the end, it's revealed that it was Alice's typewriter that typed the card. Alice was a middle child as well.

"The Possible Dream"

Written by Al Schwartz and Bill Freedman
Directed by Oscar Rudolph
Original Airdate: February 27, 1970

EPISODE 24:

Cindy unknowingly donates Marcia's diary to the *Friend in Need* organization, and Marcia wigs out because it reveals that her dream of dreams is to one day be Mrs. Desi Arnaz Jr. To cheer her up, Alice, who knows his mother's housekeeper, invites Desi Jr. to the house. In the meantime, Carol and Cindy have found the diary in a used bookstore and Marcia's in absolute heaven.

"Going, Going . . . Steady"

Written by David P. Harmon
Directed by Oscar Rudolph
Original Airdate: October 23, 1970

EPISODE 25:

Marcia flips for Harvey Klinger—you remember him—coke bottle glasses and obsessed with bugs? Anyway, he asks Marcia to go steady, and they spend the next few days drooling over larvae. Shortly thereafter, despite giving Marcia his approval, Mike decides Marcia's too young to be going steady. Not very happy about this, Marcia throws a tantrum, but she comes to her senses and the kids break up.

"The Dropout"

Written by Bill Freedman and Ben Gershman
Directed by Peter Baldwin
Original Airdate: September 25, 1970

Greg meets Los Angeles Dodger, Don Drysdale. Don says a few encouraging words to Greg, and before we know it, Greg's grades begin to slip as he becomes obsessed with becoming the next bonus baby for the Dodgers! No one can get through to Greg. But he soon learns his lesson after he's sent home from his pony league game by the coach for his oversized ego and less than stellar performance on the pitching mound.

"The Baby-sitters"

Written by Bruce Howard
Directed by Oscar Rudolph
Original Airdate: October 2, 1970

Mike surprises Carol with tickets to the theatre for the same night Alice has promised to help Sam hang curtains (yeah, right). When Greg and Marcia are left alone to baby-sit for the first time, Mike and Carol begin to have second thoughts about their competency. Cutting their dinner short, they swing by the house to sneak a peek at the kids, but Greg calls the cops when he hears strange noises out back.

"The Treasure of Sierra Avenue"

Written by Gwen Bagni and Paul Dubov
Directed by Oscar Rudolph
Original Airdate: November 6, 1970

Bobby finds eleven hundred dollars while he and the boys are playing football in a nearby parking lot. The boys think they've struck it rich . . . and unfortunately so do the girls (after all, how many times have we heard Mike's "share-and-share-alike" speech?). All too soon, we begin to hear the familiar sound of bickering in the Brady household. Mike settles this once and for all and reports it to the police. Shortly thereafter, the kindly old owner shows up on the Brady doorstep to thank the boys for turning in his wallet. He even tries to give the boys a hundred dollar reward, but they talk him down to twenty. Seems the smile on the old man's face is reward enough. *Right.*

"The Un-Underground Movie"

Written by Albert E. Lewin
Directed by Jack Arnold
Original Airdate: October 16, 1970

EPISODE 29:

Greg has to make a movie about the pilgrims for a school history project. The whole family gets involved and, per usual, Murphy's Law kicks in. The kids argue about their roles, Mike and Carol want to run the show, and Greg almost snaps! No worry, though. *Our Pilgrim Fathers* ends up a smash hit with his class and Greg gets his *A*.

"The Slumber Caper"

Written by Tam Spiva
Directed by Oscar Rudolph
Original Airdate: October 9, 1970

EPISODE 30:

Marcia has her first slumber party, but it's almost cancelled because she gets in trouble at school for something she didn't do. One of her friends wrote a nasty caption about a teacher on a drawing Marcia had done of George Washington. Quick to point the finger, Marcia blames Jenny Wilton and uninvites her from the party. In the meantime, the boys plot to ruin the party with gags and dirty tricks. The night of the party finally arrives, and once in full swing, the boys get in on the action. But amid an itching powder–induced frenzy, Marcia discovers it wasn't Jenny who framed her, but Paula Tardy.

"Confessions, Confessions"

Written by Brad Radnitz
Directed by Russ Mayberry
Original Airdate: December 18, 1970

EPISODE 31:

Peter breaks Carol's favorite vase while playing ball in the house. Afraid he'll be grounded and miss his first camping trip, the rest of the kids take the blame for him. When Mike and Carol figure out it was Peter (he was the only one who didn't confess) they guilt him into confessing by letting him dole out punishments to his brothers and sisters. After a lot of agonizing, Peter sucks it up and does what he's asked. He's home-free, but just as he's about to leave, he can't take it anymore and 'fesses up.

"The Tattletale"

EPISODE 32:

Written by Sam Locke and Milton Pascal
Directed by Russ Mayberry
Original Airdate: December 4, 1970

Cindy starts tattling and gets everyone in trouble, including Alice, whose boyfriend Sam finds out she's been hugging the postman. Cindy claims she's just telling it like it is. Cute, but no one's amused. After a lecture from Mike, she vows to never tattle again. So when Tiger runs off with Alice's prize voucher from the Everb Pressed Fabric Company jingle contest, she keeps quiet. When Alice frantically questions her about the voucher and Cindy won't tell, Carol gives her permission to tattle.

"Call Me Irresponsible"

EPISODE 33:

Written by Bruce Howard
Directed by Bill Cooper
Original Airdate: October 30, 1970

Mike puts Greg on the payroll so he can start saving for a new car. Greg's first assignment: to deliver important sketches to the

Part IV

printer. Along the way, however, Greg stops at the newsstand to check out hot rod magazines and he loses the sketches. Mike's boss wants Greg fired, but Mike talks him into giving Greg another chance. But this time, Greg has bike trouble. When his girlfriend and her father just happen by, they offer him a lift, but he leaves the sketches in the car. He is able to recover them, but not before a frantic Mike almost wears a hole in the living room carpet.

"The Impractical Joker"

EPISODE 34:

Written by Burt Styler
Directed by Oscar Rudolph
Original Airdate: January 1, 1971

Jan has herself in stitches over some silly practical jokes she's pulled on the family, one of which was to take Myron, Greg's new pet mouse, and hide him in the girls' clothes hamper. Little does she know, the mouse has gnawed its way out and Alice, who isn't aware of Greg's new pet, sees him and calls the exterminator. Fortunately, the mouse escapes the deadly fumes and takes refuge in Tiger's doghouse.

"A Fistful of Reasons"

EPISODE 35:

Written by Tam Spiva
Directed by Oscar Rudolph
Original Airdate: November 13, 1970

Cindy gets teased about her lisp by Buddy Hinton, the school bully. Peter steps in and tries reasoning with Buddy, but Buddy just belts him in the eye. After Mike and Carol try some calm, cool reasoning with Buddy's parents, who are just as bad as Buddy, Mike gives Peter permission to fight, *if* the situation calls for it. One lucky punch later, Peter knocks Buddy's tooth loose and guess who's got a lisp now!

"What Goes Up . . ."

Written by William Raynor and Myles Wilder
Directed by Leslie H. Martinson
Original Airdate: December 11, 1970

Bobby becomes a member of Peter's treehouse club, but on his way up to meet the rest of the gang, he falls and sprains his ankle. Now he's afraid of heights and the whole Brady clan join forces to help him overcome his new fear. Mike even brings a trampoline home, but no luck. It isn't until Bobby runs out back to rescue his new bird from the trees that he realizes his fear of heights is gone.

"Coming Out Party"

Written by David P. Harmon
Directed by Oscar Rudolph
Original Airdate: January 29, 1971

Mike's boss, Mr. Phillips, invites the family to go fishing, but Cindy and Carol come down with tonsillitis and they cancel the trip. In bed and not allowed to talk, the phone rings and Carol thinks it's Mike pretending to be his boss. But as soon as she refers to Mr. Phillips's boat as a broken-down barnacle barge, Mike appears at the door and she realizes her error. No harm done, though. Apparently his boss is an understanding guy because he soon appears at the Brady house with flowers.

"The Not-So-Ugly Duckling"

Written by Paul West
Directed by Irving Moore
Original Airdate: November 20, 1970

Jan finds out that her latest crush, Clark Tyson, has a thing for Marcia. Devastated, Jan makes up an imaginary boyfriend so her family won't think she's a total loser. The Bradys decide to throw Jan a surprise birthday party to cheer her up and want to invite her new boyfriend. The problem is, they can't seem to locate him. Soon after, Carol discovers that Clark isn't attracted to Jan because she dresses like one of the guys. Solution: give

Jan a makeover. In the end, Jan gets her man and her imaginary boyfriend disappears.

"Tell It Like It Is"

Written by Charles Hoffman
Directed by Terry Becker
Original Airdate: March 26, 1971

EPISODE 39:

Carol writes a story about her family for *Tomorrow's Woman* magazine. Unfortunately, the editors don't think people want to hear about the problems of having a large family, they want to hear how wonderful it is. Carol rewrites the story and this time it's accepted. But when the editors unexpectedly drop by for a visit and find the Brady household in total disarray, they reject her again. Now the senior editor wants to run Carol's first story after all.

"The Drummer Boy"

Written by Tom and Helen August
Directed by Oscar Rudolph
Original Airdate: January 22, 1971

EPISODE 40:

Bobby takes up the drums and annoys the heck out of the entire family. Although the title suggests the episode is about Bobby, it's really about Peter, whose football buddies are giving him a hard time for being in the school Glee Club. According to them, Peter's a sissy, so he quits the Glee Club. Enter Deacon Jones, defensive end for the Los Angeles Rams. Seems Deacon loves to sing. After giving the boys the old "real-men-don't-give-in-to-peer-pressure" lecture, Peter decides to remain a faithful member of the Glee Club.

"Where There's Smoke"

Written by David P. Harmon
Directed by Oscar Rudolph
Original Airdate: January 8, 1971

EPISODE 41:

Greg succumbs to peer pressure and has his first cigarette. Mike and Carol find out, but he gets off with a slap on the wrist after promising to never smoke again. Later, when a pack of cigarettes falls out of his coat pocket, questions arise and Greg is determined to clear his name (even though Mike and Carol believe him when he says they're not his). After a little detective work, Greg realizes he's got someone else's jacket, and his tarnished reputation is once again restored.

"Will the Real Jan Brady Please Stand Up?"

Written by Al Schwartz and Bill Freedman
Directed by Peter Baldwin
Original Airdate: January 15, 1971

Jan flips out (how *unusual*) because Marcia receives a birthday invitation to Lucy Winter's birthday party, which was intended for Jan. Convinced she's just another face in the crowd because all the Brady girls are blonde, Jan decides to go brunette. Empowered by her new look, Jan resists the taunts of her brothers and sisters and decides to wear her new wig to Lucy's party. Once there, the whole gang takes one look at Jan's new hairdo and laughs her all the way home. All ends well, though, as Lucy catches up to her, explaining that they all thought it had to be a joke. Why else would someone with such beautiful blonde hair cover it up?

"Our Son, the Man"

Written by Albert E. Lewin
Directed by Jack Arnold
Original Airdate: February 5, 1971

Greg moves into Mike's den, because now that he's in high school, he needs more privacy. Like a scene straight out of *Love American Style*—beads, lava lamps, peace, and love—Greg not only revamps Mike's den, he also changes his look to keep up with the changing times . . . and to impress a certain senior he's sure is interested in him. When she turns him down, he's so humiliated he sheds his groovy new image and moves back in with the boys.

"The Liberation of Marcia Brady"

Written by Charles Hoffman
Directed by Russ Mayberry
Original Airdate: February 12, 1971

Marcia speaks out for women of all ages and tells the world (okay, maybe the local viewing area) that women can do whatever men can do when a TV reporter visits her junior high school. Although the women in the Brady family applaud her bravado, the men are less than pleased. They taunt her mercilessly and Marcia gets so upset she decides to join Greg's Frontier Scouts, despite his brutish objections. Then Greg retaliates by threatening to join her Sunflower Girls. But when he discovers that he's too old to join, he somehow manages to talk Peter into it. But in the end, he chickens out and Marcia prevails.

"Lights Out"

Written by Bruce Howard
Directed by Oscar Rudolph
Original Airdate: February 19, 1971

Cindy suddenly develops a fear of the dark after witnessing the disappearing lady trick at a birthday party. Meanwhile, Peter's putting together his own magic act for his school's old-time vaudeville show and tries to show Cindy how the trick works by making Bobby disappear. Naturally, Bobby takes the opportunity to send Cindy over the edge and doesn't come back until hours later.

"The Winner"

Written by Elroy Schwartz
Directed by Robert Reed
Original Airdate: February 26, 1971

Bobby realizes he's the only Brady without a trophy after Cindy comes home from the playground bearing a trophy she won playing jacks. Bobby decides to enter any and every contest he can, from yo-yoing to selling magazine subscriptions to eating ice cream, failing each time. Luckily for him, his family is supportive. Upon returning home from an ice cream eating contest with stomach cramps and no trophy, Bobby's greeted by his brothers and sisters with their trophy for *"trying harder than anyone we know."*

"Double Parked"

Written by Skip Webster
Directed by Jack Arnold
Original Airdate: March 5, 1971

EPISODE 47:

Mike's architectural firm plans to build a new courthouse on the kids' local playground, so Carol, Alice, and the kids form a posse to overthrow City Hall. Mike's boss threatens him with his job if he doesn't call off the dogs, and Mike finds himself in the midst of a major moral dilemma. Mike saves the day when he comes up with a solution that satisfies everyone: build the courthouse at the site of the city dump.

"Alice's September Song"

Written by Elroy Schwartz
Directed by Oscar Rudolph
Original Airdate: March 12, 1971

EPISODE 48:

Alice's old boyfriend, Mark Millard, comes to town and sweeps her off her feet. He wines and dines her until Alice is convinced he's going to pop the question, but instead of a marriage proposal, Mark hits her with a business proposal. Blinded by love, Alice doesn't see what's really going on, so Mike takes it upon himself to check into Mark's background. Seems Alice's Prince Charming has a couple of other princesses scattered across the country.

"Ghost Town USA"

Written by Howard Leeds
Directed by Oscar Rudolph
Original Airdate: September 17, 1971

EPISODE 49:

The first of three episodes, the Bradys go to the Grand Canyon. Along the way, they decide to make camp in a deserted mining town where they meet grungy old prospector Zacchariah T. Brown (Jim Backus, a.k.a. Thurston Howell III), who entertains the Bradys with stories of the once-thriving boomtown. Little do they know, but the old man is convinced they're there to steal his claim (the guy's got a few screws loose), so he locks them in an old jail cell and takes off with their station wagon.

"Grand Canyon or Bust"

Written by Tam Spiva
Directed by Oscar Rudolph
Original Airdate: September 24, 1971

EPISODE 50:

The second of this three-parter, Zacchariah returns the Brady's car, and the family is, once again, back on the road headed for the Grand Canyon—this time without incident. Once at the bottom of the canyon, however, the children are warned not to wander off. Naturally, Bobby and Cindy wander off. They lose their way but meet Jimmy Pakaya, a young Indian boy who has run away from home and shows them back to camp.

"The Brady Braves"

Written by Tam Spiva
Directed by Oscar Rudolph
Original Airdate: October 10, 1971

EPISODE 51:

The last of this three-parter, Mike finds out about Jimmy and talks him into returning home. The next morning, Jimmy returns to the Brady campsite with his grandfather, Chief Dan Eagle Cloud, who invites the Bradys to a ceremony that night. During the ceremony he makes each Brady an honorary member of his tribe as his way of thanking them for bringing his grandson home.

"Juliet Is the Sun"

Written by Brad Raditz
Directed by Jack Arnold
Original Airdate: October 29, 1971

Marcia lands the lead role in *Romeo and Juliet* and drives the whole family nuts with her over-inflated ego. She even thinks she can improve on Shakespeare and rewrites her lines. Carol finally steps in and yanks Marcia from the show. After a somewhat uncharacteristic display of emotion, Marcia humbly crawls back to Carol and apologizes for being such a little snot. By now, Juliet's already been replaced so Marcia must once again humble herself and play Juliet's mother instead.

"The Wheeler Dealer"

Written by Bill Freedman and Ben Gershman
Directed by Jack Arnold
Original Airdate: October 8, 1971

Greg buys a used convertible from his *good friend* Eddie. After a little bit of elbow grease, the car looks great. The problem is, it's a lemon. An angry Greg decides turnabout is fair play, so he finds himself a sucker to unload the car on. At the last minute, however, his conscience gets the best of him and he does the right thing.

"The Personality Kid"

Written by Ben Starr
Directed by Oscar Rudolph
Original Airdate: October 22, 1971

Someone tells Peter he's dull, so at Mike's suggestion, Peter decides to *change* his personality (real good advice, Mike). When his distinguished Brit and Humphrey Bogart impressions don't fly with the family, Peter decides to become the life of the party. When he throws himself a party to try out his new personality, no one buys it and Peter learns a hard lesson about being himself. In the meantime, Bobby and Cindy are on a fire safety crusade and are now running down the stairs, blowing whistles, and screaming *"Fire"* just as Peter's finally starting to feel good about himself again.

"Her Sister's Shadow"

Written by Al Schwartz and Al Leslie
Directed by Russ Mayberry
Original Airdate: November 19, 1971

EPISODE 55:

Jan's had it with *Marcia, Marcia, Marcia!* All she hears all day is how great Marcia is at this, or how *wonderfully* Marcia does that and she sinks into a deep depression (get this girl some help, *please*). When Jan finds out she's won the *What America Means to Me* essay contest, she's overjoyed because she's finally done something Marcia's never done before. But when she discovers her score was tallied incorrectly, she toys with not telling anyone and almost goes through with accepting the award. Finally, she tells the truth and her honesty is applauded.

"The Teeter-Totter Caper"

Written by Joel Kane and Jack Lloyd
Directed by Russ Mayberry
Original Airdate: December 31, 1971

EPISODE 56:

Bobby and Cindy, tired of being excluded from certain activities because of their age, resolve to show the family they can do anything adults can do and set out to break the world teeter-tottering record. In doing so, they wind up in the newspaper, but not in any world record books—they just couldn't keep their little eyes open long enough to break the record. Mike, however, reminds them that even though they didn't break any records, they did set a record for kids their age.

"My Sister Benedict Arnold"

Written by Elroy Schwartz
Directed by Hal Cooper
Original Airdate: October 15, 1971

EPISODE 57:

Marcia invites Warren Mulaney, Greg's greatest adversary, over to help her study (Warren beat out Greg for first string on the basketball team). To get back at her, Greg invites Kathy Lawrence to the house to practice her cheers (Kathy beat out Marcia for head cheerleader). Soon the house sounds like the Fillmore Junior High football field as Kathy begins chanting the school fight song while bopping around all over the living room. Soon after, Marcia and Greg go at it, leaving Kathy and Warren alone. The ending is predicable, but happy.

"The Private Ear"

Written by Michael Morris
Directed by Hal Cooper
Original Airdate: November 12, 1971

EPISODE 58:

Peter goes around taping everyone's private conversations but gets busted after the family realizes that all the gossip originated with him. Mike lets him off with a slap on the wrist and a promise never to do it again, but this doesn't sit well with Greg and Marcia who are still pretty upset. To get back at him, they plant a phony tape on which they discuss a pretend surprise party for Peter. Peter finds the tape, but so do Mike and Carol, who decide it's Greg and Marcia who need to learn a lesson. Peter gets his surprise party and Greg and Marcia get zip.

"And Now a Word from Our Sponsor"

Written by Albert E. Lewin
Directed by Peter Baldwin
Original Airdate: November 5, 1971

EPISODE 59:

The Bradys are approached by hip director Skip Farnum, who wants them to star in a commercial for Safe laundry detergent. With no acting experience to speak of, Carol enlists the help of Myrna Carter, an aspiring actress friend of the family, to teach them the fine art of method acting. But it's more like the blind leading the blind and the shooting is a disaster.

Part IV

"Click"

Written by Tom and Helen August
Directed by Oscar Rudolph
Original Airdate: November 26, 1971

EPISODE 60:

Carol makes Greg quit the school football team after coming home with bruised ribs. Greg's bummed, but there's one consolation: He can spend more time watching the cheerleaders. At one particularly close game in which Westdale felt the refs had made a bad call, Greg happens to take a picture of one of his latest cheerleader babes. In developing the pictures, Greg notices that the play in question shows Westdale should have actually won the game. After showing the picture to the coach, Greg is made the team's official photographer.

"The Not-So-Rose-Colored Glasses"

Written by Bruce Howard
Directed by Leslie H. Martinson
Original Airdate: December 24, 1971

EPISODE 61:

Jan finds out she needs glasses, but she's certain they make her look positively goofy, so she refuses to wear them . . . until she slams her bike into the family portrait Mike has hidden away in the garage for his wedding anniversary. Now the kids have to sneak out and have another portrait taken. When Mike discovers Jan wearing her glasses in this second portrait, remembering she didn't have them on in the first one, she's busted. But all's well that ends well. When Mike discovers she sold her bike to pay for the second portrait, he's too moved to punish her.

"Little Big Man"

Written by Skip Webster
Directed by Robert Reed
Original Airdate: January 7, 1972

EPISODE 62:

Bobby's had it with people making fun of his height and decides to do something about it. From high-protein shakes to stretching himself, Bobby tries everything under the sun to get bigger, but nothing seems to be helping. Poor Bobby. Not a whole lot he can do about this one except wait it out. But Bobby soon learns that being small can be an advantage when he and Greg get trapped in Sam's meat locker, and Bobby is just small enough to climb out of the window.

"Getting Davy Jones"

Written by Phil Leslie and Al Schwartz
Directed by Oscar Rudolph
Original Airdate: December 10, 1971

EPISODE 63:

Marcia promises her junior high school she can get Davy Jones to sing at their prom. When she isn't able to make good on her promise, Marcia realizes she has to admit to the whole school that she failed. Just as she's about to make the dreaded phone call, who should appear at the Brady doorstep but Davy Jones himself to save the day (how convenient). Not only does he agree to sing at her prom, but he asks Marcia to be his date.

"Dough Re Mi"

Written by Ben Starr
Directed by Allan Barron
Original Airdate: January 14, 1972

EPISODE 64:

Greg writes his first "hit song" but doesn't have the money to record it himself, so the kids pool their money and form *The Brady Six*. Just before their scheduled recording session, however, Peter's voice begins to change, ruining the whole song. The solution: Greg simply writes another "hit song," only this one appropriately incorporates Peter's puberty.

"The Big Bet"

Written by Elroy Schwartz
Directed by Earl Bellamy
Original Airdate: January 28, 1972

EPISODE 65:

Bobby bets Greg he can do twice as many chin-ups as his brother. Bobby winds up winning and Greg has to do whatever Bobby tells him to do for a whole week. Greg draws the line, however, when Bobby demands to go along on Greg's date with Rachel (Hope Schwartz, Sherwood's daughter), except Mike gives Greg the old "no-bet's-a-sure-thing" lecture and Bobby puts on his dancing shoes. Of course, he makes a continual nuisance of himself, and the date eventually ends in catastrophe.

"Jan's Aunt Jenny"

Written by Michael Morris
Directed by Hal Cooper
Original Airdate: January 21, 1972

EPISODE 66:

Jan inches closer to the proverbial edge when she meets her great Aunt Jenny (Imogene Coca), a less than attractive woman who once looked exactly like Jan. Jan assumes she'll look just like her great aunt one day and just about loses it. Convinced she's doomed to a life of empty dance cards and dateless Saturday nights, Jan resists Aunt Jenny's attempts to get close. Jan soon discovers that although her great aunt may be a little whacked, she's a pretty cool old lady.

"Cindy Brady, Lady"

Written by Al Schwartz and Marty Rhine
Directed by Hal Cooper
Original Airdate: February 18, 1972

EPISODE 67:

Bobby pretends to be Cindy's secret admirer to make her feel more grown up like her older sisters. When Mike finds out, he orders Bobby to tell Cindy the truth. Bobby, however, has different ideas. Instead, he bribes one of his buddies to play Cindy's secret admirer. When Mike and Carol find out about Bobby's scheme, he's busted, but because his buddy ends up falling for Cindy, Mike and Carol let the whole thing go.

"The Power of the Press"

Written by Bill Freedman and Sam Gershman
Directed by Jack Arnold
Original Airdate: February 4, 1972

EPISODE 68:

Peter gets his own column in the school paper and becomes the most popular guy in school for saying nice things about his classmates. But as he spends more time on his column and collecting gifts and invitations from all his new best friends, his grades begin to suffer and he's in danger of failing science. So he writes a very flattering article about his extremely boring science teacher hoping it might help his case. Not a chance. Peter walks away with a D-minus but learns his lesson.

"Sergeant Emma"

Written by Harry Winkler
Directed by Jack Arnold
Original Airdate: February 11, 1972

EPISODE 69:

Alice's identical cousin Emma, an army drill sergeant, takes over while Alice is out of town. Performing white glove tests and leading the family in 6 A.M. workouts, the Bradys begin counting the days until Alice's return. They even plan a surprise party to welcome her home, but Emma mistakenly believes it's a going away party for her. Because Emma is obviously touched by this, the kids don't have the heart to tell her the truth.

"The Fender Benders"

Written by David P. Harmon
Directed by Allan Barron
Original Airdate: March 10, 1972

EPISODE 70:

Carol gets into a car accident with a man named Harry Duggan (Jackie Coogan, a.k.a. Uncle Fester). Claiming the accident was entirely Carol's fault, Mr. Duggan takes her to court, but Carol fights back. The two have their day in court. Carol prevails when, thanks to Mike's quick thinking, Mr. Duggan painlessly whips his head around after Mike startles him by throwing his briefcase to the ground.

"My Fair Opponent"

EPISODE 71:

Written by Bernie Kahn
Directed by Peter Baldwin
Original Airdate: March 3, 1972

Marcia transforms Molly Webber, the most unpopular girl in school, into Senior Banquet Hostess material. Her make-over is amazing and now Molly is the most popular girl in school. When Marcia also gets nominated for Senior Banquet Hostess, Molly dares Marcia to beat her. Molly wins but offers no apologies. She eventually apologizes for being such a snot and resolves the problem by suggesting they be co-hostesses.

"Hawaii Bound"

EPISODE 72:

Written by Tam Spiva
Directed by Jack Arnold
Original Airdate: September 22, 1972

The first of yet another three-parter, the Bradys go to Hawaii and Bobby finds a little tiki statue, convinced it's a good luck idol. He even gives it to Greg to wear in a surfing competition, except Greg wipes out and the family fears he's drowned.

"Pass the Tabu"

EPISODE 73:

Written by Tam Spiva
Directed by Jack Arnold
Original Airdate: September 29, 1972

The second of this three-parter, Mike saves Greg, and the boys learn that Bobby's good luck idol is really tabu. So when a tarantula crawls across Peter's chest while he's wearing the idol in bed, Bobby decides to get rid of it. They speak with Old Mr. Hanalei, an island native, who says that the only way to get rid of the tabu is to return it to the tomb of the first king at an ancient burial ground on the island. At the burial site, the boys are abducted by a nutty professor (Vincent Price).

"The Tiki Caves"

Written by Tam Spiva
Directed by Jack Arnold
Original Airdate: October 6, 1972

EPISODE 74:

The boys are held captive by nutty Professor Whitehead because he's convinced they have stolen the idol from his cave where he's been searching for such island treasures. He ties them all up so he can claim the idol as his own discovery. In the meantime, the girls begin to worry when the boys don't return and finally tell Mike and Carol where they've gone. Concerned, they go to the burial ground where they find and rescue their sons.

"Today I Am a Freshman"

Written by William Raynor and Myles Wilder
Directed by Hal Cooper
Original Airdate: October 13, 1972

EPISODE 75:

Marcia's so afraid of not being popular when she goes to high school that she joins every club in school, one of which is the Booster Club. Meanwhile, Peter joins the science club and is building a miniature volcano on the back patio. Marcia invites the Booster Club to the Brady house for her first meeting, but things come to a screeching halt when Peter's volcano erupts all over the Boosters. Marcia thinks it's funny, but the Boosters don't share her sense of humor and Marcia gets the boot, but not without a good laugh.

"Cyrano De Brady"

Written by Skip Webster
Directed by Hal Cooper
Original Airdate: October 20, 1972

EPISODE 76:

Peter falls head over heals for Jan's new friend, Kerry Hathaway. Because Peter gets tongue-tied when he sees her, Greg helps by feeding Peter romantic lines while Peter stands outside her bedroom window. When Kerry discovers Greg in the bushes, she misunderstands and falls for him instead.

Part IV

Greg tries to scare her off by playing male slut, but Peter can't stand seeing Kerry so hurt and he blows his cover. Impressed with Peter's sincerity, Kerry dumps Greg and falls for Peter.

"Fright Night"

Written by Brad Radnitz
Directed by Jerry London
Original Airdate: October 27, 1972

Alice claims she's not afraid of anything so the kids decide to put her to the test and plan to scare her while Mike and Carol are out the following Friday night. Alice ends up eating her words, but the kids end up the real losers after Alice, thinking there's an intruder in the house, smashes Mike's head into a million little pieces. Relax, it's only Carol's sculpture.

"Career Fever"

Written by Burt and Adele Styler
Directed by Jerry London
Original Airdate: November 17, 1972

Mike mistakenly thinks Greg wants to be an architect after reading a paper Greg wrote for school. Greg doesn't have the heart to tell him he wrote the paper only because he couldn't think of anything else to write. Greg thinks all he has to do is create something awful and Mike will have to tell Greg he shouldn't be an architect. Meanwhile, Peter decides he wants to be a doctor, but after studying a doctor's disease manual, he's convinced he's dying of an incurable illness. As usual, all's well that ends well. Greg doesn't have to be an architect and Peter isn't dying after all.

"Law and Disorder"

Written by Elroy Schwartz
Directed by Hal Cooper
Original Airdate: January 12, 1973

Bobby becomes a school safety monitor and decides to be the best safety monitor that ever lived. No one at Clinton

Elementary School will run in the halls or chew gum on the premises again. His friends at school begin dropping like flies, and Bobby doesn't realize just how unpopular he's become until it's too late. Finally, Bobby's forced to compromise his integrity when a little girl asks him to rescue her cat from a condemned building. In doing so, he winds up getting in a little trouble for once.

"Jan, the Only Child"

Written by Al Schwartz and Ralph Goodman
Directed by Roger Duchowney
Original Airdate: November 11, 1972

EPISODE 80:

Jan, once again, goes completely wacko and announces to the family that she wishes she were an only child. Sensitive to her neuroses, the kids try everything from respecting her privacy to giving her some space. Jan, however, doesn't appreciate their efforts so they grant her wish and play invisible. They don't even talk to her anymore. In the end, Jan's had it with the silent treatment and apologizes to everyone and rejoins the family.

"The Show Must Go On"

Written by Harry Winkler
Directed by Jack Donohue
Original Airdate: November 3, 1972

EPISODE 81:

Greg and Marcia talk Mike and Carol into performing with them in the Westdale High Family Frolic Night. Carol and Marcia plan to sing a duet from the musical *Gypsy*, and Mike plans to read Henry Wadsworth Longfellow while Greg strums along on the guitar. Alice and Sam are fighting because Sam has plans the night of the show, and the girls plot to get them back together by making Sam jealous. Sam falls for it and the two reunite. Frolic Night is a hit and the Brady family steals the show.

"You Can't Win 'Em All"

Written by Lois Hire
Directed by Jack Donohue
Original Airdate: March 16, 1973

EPISODE 82:

Bobby and Cindy are both up to compete on the "Question the Kids Show", provided they pass the qualifying exam. Cindy studies her butt off, but Bobby doesn't think he needs to. When Cindy passes and Bobby doesn't, she develops a little ego problem that's got everyone hot under the collar and no one can stand to be around her. But in addition to suffering from an enlarged ego, Cindy also suffers from stage fright and blows the competition.

"Goodbye, Alice, Hello"

Written by Milt Rosen
Directed by George "Buddy" Tyne
Original Airdate: November 24, 1972

EPISODE 83:

The kids accuse Alice of squealing after each gets busted for one thing or another and they give her the cold shoulder. It finally gets to be too much for her so she leaves the Bradys and takes a job at a local diner across town. She recruits her friend Kay to be her replacement, but the kids quickly realize Alice can't be easily replaced, especially when they discover that Kay has the personality of a wet shoe. Soon enough, the kids are begging Alice to come home.

"Love and the Older Man"

Written by Martin A. Ragaway
Directed by George "Buddy" Tyne
Original Airdate: January 5, 1973

EPISODE 84:

Marcia falls for her hot new dentist, Dr. Stanley Vogel, and her libido switches into overdrive as she fantasizes about becoming Mrs. Marcia Dentist. But all her dreams come crashing down when Jan informs her that he's already married. Marcia, believing he's interested in her, tells Dr. Vogel they must never see each other again. Fortunately, Mike fills Dr. Vogel in on Marcia's lastest crush and he plays along to save her the embarrassment.

"Everyone Can't Be George Washington"

Written by Sam Locke and Milton Pascal
Directed by Richard Michaels
Original Airdate: December 22, 1972

Peter tries out for the part of George Washington in the school play, but winds up with the role of Benedict Arnold. Peter takes a lot of razzing from his classmates about being a traitor, and having had enough of it, he decides to quit the play. After a heart to heart with Mike and Carol, Peter realizes just how important he is to the success of the play and decides he's going to be the *best* Benedict Arnold his school has ever seen. The show's a success and Peter's a hit.

"Greg's Triangle"

Written by Bill Freedman and Ben Gershman
Directed by Richard Michaels
Original Airdate: December 8, 1972

Greg is chairman of the head cheerleader selection committee and both Marcia *and* his new girlfriend want to be head cheerleader. To make matters worse, there's a three-way tie, and Greg must cast the deciding vote. After giving it some serious consideration, Greg doesn't vote for either of them; he votes for Pat Conway (Rita Wilson) because he really believes she's the best. Marcia takes it like a man; but his girlfriend is a different story. After she hangs up on him, Greg finally comes to the conclusion that *possibly, just possibly,* she was just using him to get his vote.

"Bobby's Hero"

Written by Michael Morris
Directed by Leslie H. Martinson
Original Airdate: February 16, 1973

Bobby, for some twisted reason, picks Jesse James as his hero for a school paper he has to write. Concerned by this, Mike and Carol bring home some books on Jesse James, hoping to enlighten Bobby to the evils of this man. They even invite a man whose family was killed by Jesse James to the house to talk to Bobby. Nothing seems to sink in, however, until Bobby has a nightmare about his own family being taken out by Jesse James, one by one, while he stands by and watches.

"The Great Earring Caper"

Written by Larry Rhine and Al Schwartz
Directed by Leslie H. Martinson
Original Airdate: March 2, 1973

Cindy loses a pair of Carol's favorite earrings and enlists Peter's help to find them. The two of them search high and low, but to no avail. Meanwhile, Carol wants the earrings and Cindy is forced to come clean. The next thing we know, the entire Brady family is retracing the moments of the afternoon the earrings disappeared as just about everyone had a hand in their disappearance. They finally discover the mangled earrings in the washing machine.

"Greg Gets Grounded"

Written by Elroy Schwartz
Directed by Jack Arnold
Original Airdate: January 19, 1973

Greg gets grounded from the family car for one week. He's bummed because now he can't go buy concert tickets. After a little brainstorming, Greg realizes Mike banned him from the family car, not *all* cars, so he borrows a buddy's car. When Mike finds out, he blows a gasket. In his own defense, Greg quotes Mike's exact words and there's no argument. Mike relents but vows to live by Greg's exact words in the future. So when Greg promises his brothers he'll drive them to a frog-jumping contest the same night he has a date with Rachel (Hope Schwartz), let's just say the frogs see more action than Greg does.

"The Subject Was Noses"

Written by Al Schwartz and Larry Rhine
Directed by Jack Arnold
Original Airdate: February 9, 1973

EPISODE 90:

Marcia gets nailed in the nose by a football after breaking her date with Charley to go out with Doug Simpson. But when Doug takes one look at her swollen nose, he breaks his date with her (even Marcia Brady's not immune from karma) and she's devastated. But who should be nearby, waiting on the sidelines but Charley. Marcia tells him what happened and then confesses that she lied to him. Charley takes it like a man, but succumbs to her wily charms and gives her a second chance.

"How to Succeed in Business"

Written by Gene Thompson
Directed by Robert Reed
Original Airdate: February 23, 1973

EPISODE 91:

Peter gets his first job at Mr. Martinelli's bicycle repair shop but gets fired after just three days because he's not mechanically inclined. Peter goes home and tells Greg the news and begs him not to tell Mike and Carol. But the family, who's under the mistaken impression that Peter has just gotten a promotion, throws him a party to celebrate. Soon after, Mike and Carol discover the truth and prompt Peter to come clean.

"Amateur Nite"

Written by Sam Locke and Milton Pascal
Directed by Jack Arnold
Original Airdate: January 26, 1973

EPISODE 92:

Jan almost blows *another* anniversary after secretly ordering engraving for the silver platter the kids bought for their parents.

Part IV

Not realizing it cost eighty-five cents per letter, not for the whole engraving (come on, Jan . . .), the kids don't have enough money to pay for it. So Jan signs them up for a televised talent contest in which first prize is a hundred bucks. The kids secretly put together a routine, make the cut, and call themselves the *Silver Platters*. They come in third and go home, only to find that Mike and Carol have already paid for the platter.

"You're Never Too Old"

Written by Ben Gershman and Bill Freedman
Directed by Bruce Bilson
Original Airdate: March 9, 1973

EPISODE 93:

Carol's grandmother, Connie Hutchins (Florence Henderson), comes to town for a visit and the girls decide to fix her up with Great Grandpa Brady (Robert Reed). But there's a problem, Connie's got the spirit of an eighteen-year-old and Hank (a retired judge) may as well be dead. The two hit it off like fire and gasoline, and the night ends in total disaster. Fortunately, as the old saying goes, "opposites attract," and before the episode's end, the two are off to the Little White Chapel in Las Vegas.

"A Room at the Top"

Written by William Raynor and Myles Wilder
Directed by Lloyd Schwartz
Original Airdate: March 23, 1973

EPISODE 94:

Mike unknowingly promises Greg the attic at the same time Carol promises it to Marcia. After some tearful deliberation, Greg gets the attic because he's the oldest. Marcia tries to make him feel sorry for her and succeeds, but Peter and Bobby want Greg out of their room. They set out to make Marcia's life miserable by showing her how difficult life can be, having to climb *all* those stairs. In the end, Marcia turns the attic back over to Greg and apologizes for being such a blubbering idiot about the whole thing.

"Snow White and the Seven Bradys"

Written by Ben Starr
Directed by Bruce Bilson
Original Airdate: September 28, 1973

EPISODE 95:

The Bradys put on a production of *Snow White and the Seven Dwarfs* in their backyard to raise money to buy Cindy's retiring teacher, Mrs. Whitfield, a set of first edition books. After a few minor catastrophes, such as Cindy not securing a theatre, the cops haul Mike off to the station just before curtain call for not having a permit to have the show in the Brady's backyard. Fortunately for everyone, Mike gets back before Mrs. Whitfield passes out from the heat. The play is a hit and we have yet another happy ending.

"Mail Order Hero"

Written by Martin A. Ragaway
Directed by Bruce Bilson
Original Airdate: September 28, 1973

EPISODE 96:

Bobby, engaged in one-upmanship with his buddies, tells them that Joe Namath is a good friend of his. Of course, no one believes him . . . probably because Bobby doesn't know the man. Then Cindy comes up with a plan and writes Joe a letter claiming to be a very, very sick Bobby. Joe gets the letter and goes to the Brady house to see him before it's too late. Bobby almost gets away with it, but he comes clean. Joe is flattered and even sticks around to throw a few passes with Bobby and his friends.

"The Elopement"

Written by Harry Winkler
Directed by Jerry London
Original Airdate: December 7, 1973

EPISODE 97:

The Brady family thinks Alice and Sam are planning to elope after witnessing a series of mysterious conversations between the two lovers. When Alice and Sam return home after a bowling date, they're greeted by streamers, balloons, and a bunch of screaming Bradys. After feeling like a bunch of idiots, Mike humbly admits they simply jumped to conclusions.

"Adios, Johnny Bravo"

Written by Joanna Lee
Directed by Jerry London
Original Airdate: September 14, 1973

EPISODE 98:

Greg is discovered by a talent agent who wants to turn him into the new *Johnny Bravo!* Greg takes the bait and agrees to sign with the agency. When he announces to his parents that he's decided not to attend college, Mike gives him the old "an-education-is-a-good-thing-to-fall-back-on" lecture, only Greg can't see past his new shades. Soon enough, Greg discovers the only reason the agent wanted him was because he fit the suit (an expensive jacket the company invested in for the next *Johnny Bravo*).

"Never Too Young"

Written by Al Schwartz and Larry Rhine
Directed by Richard Michaels
Original Airdate: October 5, 1973

EPISODE 99:

Bobby gets kissed by Millicent (Melissa Sue Anderson, a.k.a. Mary Ingalls), but soon finds out he may have been exposed to the mumps. To make matters worse, Cindy happens to see the kiss and tells everyone she has a secret. Poor Bobby. He was just looking for a little action and look what happens. Afraid to tell anyone he kissed a girl, Bobby stays away from the family until he finds out whether Millicent actually has the mumps.

"Peter and the Wolf"

Written by Tam Spiva
Directed by Leslie H. Martinson
Original Airdate: October 12, 1973

EPISODE 100:

Peter pretends to be an older man so he can double date with Greg. He changes his name to Phil Packer, dons a false mustache, and drops his voice a few octaves. All goes well until "Phil" eats his mustache, Greg calls him Peter, and the girls catch on. But they play along, vowing to get even. When they go on their next date, the girls drool all over "Phil" while Greg just sits there in a huff. When Mike and Carol, who happen to be at the same restaurant with clients, catch sight of them, the jig is up.

"Getting Greg's Goat"

Written by Milton Pascal and Same Locke
Directed by Robert Reed
Original Airdate: October 19, 1973

EPISODE 101:

Greg and his buddies steal Coolidge High's mascot (a goat named Raquel) and Greg volunteers to keep her in his attic room for the weekend. When Mike thinks Greg's hiding a girl up there, Greg has to come clean. Meanwhile, Carol has invited the PTA to the Brady house for an emergency meeting to discuss how they plan to handle the recent rash of mascot stealing, and Greg is forced to keep Raquel in his room until they're all gone. When Raquel gets out, all hell breaks loose, and Greg's busted.

"The Cincinnati Kids"

Written by Al Schwartz and Larry Rhine
Directed by Leslie H. Martinson
Original Airdate: November 23, 1973

EPISODE 102:

Mike takes the family along to King's Island Amusement Park on a business trip. Everyone's having a ball until Jan starts whining about having to carry around the poster she's just bought. So Mike gives her a cylinder that is identical to the one he's carrying containing the important plans he'll be presenting that afternoon at his business meeting. Problem solved? Not quite. Jan takes off with the wrong cylinder and Mike's left with a poster of Yogi Bear. After a lot of running around, the plans finally make their way back to the right hands just in the nick of time.

"Quarterback Sneak"

Written by Ben Gershman and Bill Freedman
Directed by Peter Baldwin
Original Airdate: November 9, 1973

EPISODE 103:

Marcia goes out with Jerry Rogers, a gorgeous Westdale High football rival (and "Fairview Fink"). Greg warns Marcia that he's only using her to get his hands on Greg's playbook, but Marcia doesn't buy it, so Greg sets him up. Sure enough, he takes the bait . . . a phony playbook. When Greg tries to tell Jerry the book's a fake, he denies even taking it. And when Jerry's coach finds out about the phony playbook, he's ejected from the game and Westdale wins fair and square.

"Marcia Gets Creamed"

Written by Ben Gershman and Bill Freedman
Directed by Peter Baldwin
Original Airdate: October 26, 1973

EPISODE 104:

Marcia gets an after-school job at Haskell's Ice Cream Hut and convinces Mr. Haskell to hire Peter as well. Marcia realizes Peter's useless and fires him. Then she convinces her boss to give Jan a try. Jan works out great and Mr. Haskell is quite pleased. But when he decides he really needs only one Brady, he fires Marcia and keeps Jan. No problem. Now Marcia can spend more time with her boyfriend (Michael Gray, a.k.a. the guy who turns into SHAZAM) who has been feeling a little neglected lately.

"My Brother's Keeper"

Written by Michael Morris
Directed by Ross Bowman
Original Airdate: November 2, 1973

EPISODE 105:

Bobby saves Peter's life and Peter makes a solemn promise to be Bobby's personal slave for the rest of his life. Bobby takes total advantage of this, and pretty soon, Peter's had it. He and Bobby have it out and eventually resolve the problem by dividing the bedroom in two with a strip of masking tape.

When Bobby rips the tape, Peter chases him into the closet and Bobby freaks out when he finds himself locked in. Eventually, Peter lets him out and an overly dramatic Bobby thanks Peter for saving his life and the two make up.

"Try, Try Again"

Written by Al Schwartz and Larry Rhine
Directed by George "Buddy" Tyne
Original Airdate: November 16, 1973

Jan decides to drop ballet and take up tap dancing. Big mistake. She's even worse than she was at ballet! After announcing to the family that she's a failure at everything, Mike and Carol give her the old "if-at-first-you-don't-succeed" lecture and Jan keeps trying. Finally, after trying just about everything, it's discovered that Jan is an artist at heart. No wonder she's so neurotic.

"Kelly's Kids"

Written by Sherwood Schwartz
Directed by Richard Michaels
Original Airdate: January 4, 1974

Ken and Kathy Kelly (Ken Berry and Brooke Bundy) have moved in next door to the Bradys along with their newly adopted boy, Matt (Todd Lookinland, a.k.a. Bobby's real life little brother). Everything's wonderful until Matt starts to miss his two best friends from the orphanage. So the Kellys surprise Matt by adopting Dwayne and Steve. At first, the Kellys are taken aback when they discover that Dwayne is African American and Steve is Asian. But by the next afternoon, they're all one big happy family (yes, just like that).

"The Driver's Seat"

Written by George Tibbles
Directed by Jack Arnold
Original Airdate: January 11, 1974

Greg gives Marcia a hard time about women drivers so the two decide to settle their dispute with an obstacle course.

Remember the egg on top of the cone? Marcia gets about a half an inch away from scrambled eggs, but Greg hits the gas instead of the brakes and finishes the job. Meanwhile, Jan is suffering from panic attacks as she prepares for her second Debate Club debate after majorly messing up her first one. Mike suggests she picture the audience in their underwear to alleviate her anxiety.

"Miss Popularity"

Written by Martin Ragaway
Directed by Jack Donohue
Original Airdate: December 21, 1973

EPISODE 109:

Jan is elected "Most Popular Girl in Her Class," but soon after, Jan becomes the most *unpopular* girl in her class after welching out on all of her campaign promises. But her ego's too big to see what's really going on, and finally Mike and Carol sit her down and give her the "you-never-make-a-promise-unless-you-intend-to-keep-it" lecture. At the same time, Mike and Carol are trying to get out of town on a second honeymoon, but because of Jan's ever-shifting moods, they've got to stay put. After seeing the error of her ways, Jan turns around and promises her family and her classmates that she intends to keep every promise she ever made.

"Out of This World"

Written by Al Schwartz and Larry Rhine
Directed by Peter Baldwin
Original Airdate: January 18, 1974

EPISODE 110:

Peter and Bobby think they've seen a UFO and convince Mike and Carol to let them sleep in the backyard the next night, when the two catch sight of the cigar-shaped object and capture it on film. Carol develops the pictures, and sure enough, it looks like a real live UFO. The Bradys call in the United States Air Force to look at the pictures, unaware that the UFO is really a little scheme concocted by Greg to get even with his brothers for getting him in trouble. When someone comes to the Brady house to check it out, though, Greg is forced to tell the truth.

"Two Petes in a Pod"

Written by Sam Locke and Milton Pascal
Directed by Richard Michaels
Original Airdate: February 8, 1974

EPISODE 111:

Peter meets his double, Arthur Owens (Christopher Knight), who looks exactly like Peter except for his glasses. The boys have a lot of fun fooling everyone until Peter winds up with two dates for the same night. No problem. Peter keeps his date with Michelle while Arthur keeps his date with Pamela. But when Peter has to entertain two dates at the same time without either of them seeing the other because Arthur's late, chaos ensues and Peter has a lot of explaining to do.

"Welcome Aboard"

EPISODE 112:

Written by Al Schwartz and Larry Rhine
Directed by Richard Michaels
Original Airdate: January 25, 1974

Carol's nephew Oliver (Robby Rist) moves in, but when a series of accidents occur the minute he arrives, everyone's convinced he's a jinx. Then, when he goes along on a movie studio tour and is the one millionth visitor to pass through the gates, his luck begins to change! Thanks to Oliver, the whole family gets to appear in a real movie. In turn-of-the-century costumes, the whole family gets involved in the collision of two pie delivery trucks, and before you know it, pies are flying everywhere and Oliver becomes a member of the family.

"The Snooperstar"

EPISODE 113:

Written by Harry Winkler
Directed by Bruce Bilson
Original Airdate: February 22, 1974

Marcia suspects Cindy's been reading her diary and sets her up by writing about a talent agent who's coming over to the house to meet with Cindy about becoming the new Shirley Temple.

Part IV

Penelope Fletcher (Natalie Schafer, a.k.a. Lovey Howell), a "difficult" client of Mike's, has arrived at the Brady house and Cindy's convinced she's the agent! Bounding down the stairs in pin curls and ruffles, Cindy begins her audition, and Penelope, who hasn't cracked a smile the entire episode, is soon singing and dancing to "The Good Ship Lollypop."

"The Hustler"

Written by Bill Freedman and Ben Gershman
Directed by Michael Kane
Original Airdate: March 1, 1974

EPISODE 114:

Mike's boss, Mr. Matthews (Jim Backus, a.k.a. Zacchariah T. Brown, a.k.a. Thurston Howell III), gives Mike a brand new pool table as a bonus for a job well done. Bobby loves it because he's better than anyone else. Meanwhile, Carol's been trying to plan a small dinner party for Mr. Matthews and his wife. The problem is, Mr. Matthews keeps switching the night and inviting more people! Eventually they settle on an evening and as soon as the guests arrive, Mr. Matthews shuffles them all out back to shoot a game of pool. Bobby joins in and surprising Mr. Matthews, he makes a bet and wins. His prize? A case of chewing gum.

"Top Secret"

Written by Howard Ostroff
Directed by Bernard Wiesen
Original Airdate: February 15, 1974

EPISODE 115:

Bobby and Oliver are convinced that Mike's working for the FBI. They also think Sam's a double-agent trying to steal government plans from Mike after they catch him removing an envelope from Mike's desk (Sam's asked Mike to draw plans to expand his butcher shop). Alice thinks Mike's top-secret business with Sam is designing Sam and Alice's home. Carol and the girls are convinced of this as well and start shopping for wedding gifts. In the end, the whole thing blows up in everyone's faces and the truth comes out.

"The Hair-Brained Scheme"

Written by Chuck Stewart Jr.
Directed by Jack Arnold
Original Airdate: March 8, 1974

EPISODE 116:

In this final episode, Bobby turns entrepreneur and tries selling *Neat & Natural Hair Tonic* door-to-door hoping to make a million dollars. Failing miserably on his first day, Greg tries to pick up his spirits by buying a bottle and Bobby talks him into using it right away. The result? Bright orange hair! Greg is ready to kill Bobby because in twenty-four hours he'll be graduating from high school . . . with orange hair! Carol, however, comes to the rescue with a solution: go to the beauty parlor and have his hair dyed back to its original color. The next day, Greg graduates, and this marks the end of an era, but the beginning of re-runmania.

About the Author

Lauren Johnson is not only a walking encyclopedia of useless information, she's also a registered art therapist with a master's degree in art therapy. Lauren's been working with the mentally ill since 1990, educating her patients on the therapeutic benefit of nurturing creativity in the pursuit of personal development. At the same time that she began working in psychiatry she also started writing *Brady Bunch* trivia questions as a means of cultivating her own creativity. In the course of ten years she has compiled more than 4,000 questions. In addition to writing silly stuff like this, she is also a screenwriter. Born and raised in the western suburbs of Chicago, she now resides in Los Angeles. This is her first book.

Kirsten Johnson

Lauren Johnson with Sherwood Schwartz

The Bradys uncensored and on stage?!? FAR OUT!

Brady Home Movies

VHS	R3 #970000	$14.95
DVD	R2 #970000	$19.95

Produced by Susan Olsen (Cindy), *Brady Home Movies* originally aired on CBS, receiving phenomenal ratings. This re-edited one-hour special contains vintage footage shot by cast members on Super 8 cameras given to them by Robert Reed. Includes exclusive interviews with the cast, details on the infamous date with Barry Williams and Florence Henderson, and a touching special tribute to Robert Reed, who died from AIDS complications in 1992.

The Brady Bunch Variety Hour

VHS Vol. 1	R3 #972745	$14.95
VHS Vol. 2	R3 #972746	$14.95
VHS Vol. 1&2	R3 #972747	$24.95
DVD Vol. 1&2	R2 #976642	$19.95

Originally aired on ABC, *The Brady Bunch Variety Hour* showcased the Brady family in a new setting: the stage. For their first show, they open with the musical number "Baby Face." The kids plot to replace Mike, who is accused of "stinking up the act." Guests include Donny and Marie Osmond, Tony Randall, and Ann B. Davis.

    The second episode features the Brady crew opening with the hip-swinging number "Sunny Side Up." Greg announces he's moving out, only to discover that his plans didn't exactly turn out they way he expected. Guests include Vincent Price, Rip Taylor, and H.R. Pufnstuf.

Available wherever video and DVD are sold